# Housing policy and vulnerable social groups

Report and guidelines
prepared by the Group of Specialists
on Housing Policies for Social Cohesion (CS-HO)

French edition:

*Accès au logement des groupes vulnérables*

ISBN 978-92-871-6300-4

Council of Europe Publishing
F-67075 Strasbourg Cedex
http://book.coe.int

ISBN 978-92-871-6301-1
© Council of Europe, May 2008
Printed at the Council of Europe

The report and guidelines are the result of the meetings and contributions of the Group of Specialists on Housing Policies for Social Cohesion (CS-HO) and of a background study (*Housing subsidies supporting low-income households: A review of international experiences*, prepared for Directorate General III – Social Cohesion, Social Policy Department).

# Contents

# 1. Introduction: objective of the report

The purpose of the report is to contribute to efforts directed towards improving the access to housing of vulnerable social groups in Europe and the developing countries. The Revised European Social Charter gave special emphasis to the housing problems of vulnerable social groups,[1] which were reinforced by the Revised Strategy for Social Cohesion. There was a decision by the European Committee for Social Cohesion (CDCS) to "extend its work on access to housing, with a particular concentration on those member states where housing problems are especially acute."

The Group of Specialists on Housing Policies for Social Cohesion (CS-HO) was set up to work on improving access to housing for vulnerable groups, focusing on:

- increasing the supply of decent and affordable housing;
- facilitating access to housing finance for vulnerable groups;
- making effective use of housing allowances.

The objective of the report is to take stock of existing work in this field and summarise the best practices, thereby strengthening social cohesion by facilitating access to housing for the most vulnerable groups. On the basis of the report, the CS-HO will develop policy guidelines on promoting access to housing through sound public policies in this field, with a view to preparing a recommendation. We will also develop methodological material designed to promote the guidelines and best practices among the target groups of policy makers, involved parties and final beneficiaries.

Through this project, the CS-HO would like to make a contribution to achieving the aim defined in Article 31 of the European Social Charter (ESC). This states that housing is a human right and asks the relevant countries to "prevent and reduce homelessness with a view to its gradual elimination". The ESC requires those countries to take measures to secure the protection of persons who are not yet homeless, but may become so.

---

1. Article 31 of the Revised European Social Charter recognises the right to housing; and Article 16 provides for the protection of family life through the provision of family housing; Article 19 § 4 guarantees accommodation to migrant workers by the contracting party that is no less favourable than that guaranteed to their own nationals; and Article 4 of the Protocol stipulates that elderly persons should be provided with housing suited to their needs and their state of health, or with adequate support for adapting their housing.

## 2. Housing policy context

### 2.1. Main trends in housing policies

European housing policies went through different stages after the Second World War. In the 1940s, the emphasis was on reconstructing housing damaged during the war. The main legal and financial tools were not changed: rent control and the basic institutional and organisational framework remained untouched. In the 1950s and 1960s, the emphasis shifted to investment in new social housing, where each national government based these policies on their unique organisational structure: in the United Kingdom, municipalities played the most important role; in the Netherlands, housing associations; in Sweden, municipal companies; in France, special public-private organisations (HLM companies), etc. In the 1970s and 1980s, deregulation, privatisation and the growth of the private sector took place, and housing policy moved towards the support of the owner-occupied sector, as opposed to the social sector. Beside some general tendencies (such as shifts from supply-side subsidies towards demand-side subsidies, from direct public provision towards a kind of public-private partnership, and from specialist housing finance institutions towards the universal bank system), there are very few common elements in the housing policies of the European countries (Balchin, 1996; Harloe, 1995; Donnison and Ungerson, 1982; Lowe, 2004; Maclennan et al., 1998). The reason lies in historical differences in the emergence of the institutional structure of housing policies.

Integration through the EU has brought about a change in housing policies. There are certain trends towards the conversion of housing policies, but this will be quite a long process. The EU does not have a housing policy competence, but it does have a major impact on the housing system in each member state. In the housing finance and taxation systems there are some efforts towards integration. For example, a common market for home loan products across Europe is a key part of the EU vision for integrated retail financial markets. Maclennan et al. (1998) argue that, despite convergence pressures, differences in housing and financial market institutions across the EU member states are still enormous. This study demonstrates that the rigidities of both social housing and national housing markets could impede the transmission mechanism by which the EU economy responds to economic shocks. The paper concludes with a set of proposals for institutional reforms that would significantly reduce the tensions within the Economic Monetary Union (EMU) and the potential for instability in these economies as a result of their EMU membership. (Gibb, 2002)

According to a recent European Central Bank report (ECB, 2003) there has been no general trend in the last decade in the development of housing policies in EU member states. Many EU countries have reduced the heavy subsidies they granted to housing investment, or have restricted tax exemption related to mortgage interest payments. For instance, Sweden decided at the beginning of the 1990s to reduce the incentives to invest in immovable property, by equalising marginal tax rates across types of assets (including taxation of financial assets). Moreover, the introduction or gradual increase of real-estate taxes has further contributed to reducing some of the distortions in favour of immovable property in those countries, where the tax system had to be brought closer to a neutral system. This trend has gained speed in the second half of the 1990s, in line with the general trend towards budget consolidation (ECB, 2003).

In the housing sector of developing countries, there has been a trend since the 1970s to move away from traditional supply-side assistance to demand-side subsidies. Traditional supply-side housing programmes include government-built public housing and other so-called "bricks and mortar" subsidies given to the producers of housing such as subsidised financing, contributions of land and materials, and tax credits and deductions. If a programme is to be efficient in situations without equilibrium, it's a prerequisite that producers pass on part of the subsidy to households by charging below-market rents for the units that they produce. If it is not demanded, the subsidy will most probably become capitalised. Nevertheless, in case of market equilibrium, the increased supply will itself drive the prices down.

From the perspective of households, the key characteristic of any supply-side housing programme is lack of choice: a household must take or leave what the producer offers. In contrast, demand-side housing programmes channel subsidies directly to the household through cash-like allowances or grants. Typically, the household pays the market price and is allowed to select its home from a variety of suppliers. One characteristic of this process has been that government-controlled agencies withdrew from direct subsidising and lending in favour of provision for private lending practice (Dübel, 2000). In market economies, demand-side subsidies have been used to increase the transparency and effectiveness of subsidies (Katsura and Romanik, 2002).

Generally there is a trend away from direct provision towards an enabling role. The World Bank programmes heavily supported this policy, but changes in national policies facilitate this trend as well:

"Governments should be encouraged to adopt policies that enable housing markets to work. Governments have at their disposal seven major enabling instruments, three that address demand-side constraints, three that address supply-side constraints, and one that improves the management of the housing sector as a whole. The three demand-side tools are: (i) developing property rights: ensuring that the right to own and freely exchange housing is established by law and enforced, and administering programmes of land and house registration and regulation of insecure tenure; (ii) developing mortgage finance: creating healthy and competitive mortgage lending institutions, and fostering innovative arrangements for providing greater access to housing finance by the poor; and (iii) rationalising subsidies: ensuring that subsidy programmes are of an appropriate and affordable scale, well-targeted, measurable, and transparent, and avoid distorting housing markets.[2]

The three supply-side instruments are: (i) providing infrastructure for residential land development: co-ordinating the agencies responsible for provision of residential infrastructure (roads, drainage, water, sewage, and electricity) in order to focus on servicing existing and undeveloped urban land for efficient residential development; (ii) regulating land and housing development: balancing the costs and the benefits of regulations that influence urban land and housing markets, especially land use and building, and removing regulations which unnecessarily hinder housing supply; and (iii) organising the building industry: creating greater competition in the building industry, removing constraints to the development and use of local building materials, and reducing trade barriers that apply to housing inputs.

These instruments are to be supported and guided by developing the institutional framework for managing the housing sector. This includes strengthening the institutions which can oversee and manage the performance of the sector as a whole; bringing together all the major public agencies, private sector, and representatives of non-governmental organisations (NGOs) and community-based organisations; and ensuring that policies and programmes benefit the poor and elicit their participation."[3]

---

2. The recommendation at this point lists a number of elements, which are not compatible if we take in account the effect of external costs.
3. http://www.worldbank.org/urban/housing/hpp.htm.

The privatisation of council housing in the United Kingdom, and increased support for housing associations represent this trend in the 1980s (Lowe, 2004). The other sign of the states' withdrawal as direct providers is that public funds for mortgages were replaced in several countries, for example Finland and Sweden (Asselin et al., 2002; Boelhouwer and Elsinga, 2002). Another example is a shift in the role of the housing associations in Holland (Priemus, 2003) and in Denmark (Enberg, 2000).

To summarise, two inter-related trends can be traced in the housing policies of the developed countries in the last three decades: (i) a shift from supply-side subsides towards demand-side subsidies, and (ii) a change in the role of the state, from a direct service provider to an "enabling role". However, changes in national housing policies have occurred gradually, and several elements of the institutional and financial structure of housing policy remain alive, such as direct supply-side subsidies in France and Austria. Many countries also use both housing allowance and aids to bricks and mortar in variable proportions. In France, for instance, the balance is three-quarters housing allowance, to one-quarter aid to bricks and mortar (Taffin, 2003).

## 2.2. Trend from general to specific programmes

The severe housing shortage decreased by the end of the 1960s, and the housing policies in developed countries started to consider the problems of special social (vulnerable) groups. There are numerous ways of defining vulnerable groups, which usually differ from country to country. Nevertheless, some characteristic groups can be identified. These include geographic area – as poor houses tend be segregated; age (the elderly); demographic characteristics (one-parent households); income groups (low-income households); and ethnic minorities.

The urban ghettos in the United States (from the 1970s), run-down inner cities, and later the pauperised "high rise" housing estates have been targeted by housing programmes (area-based initiatives). After decades of housing shortages (until the end of 1960s), the problem of the mismatch between the housing supply and housing demand has gained importance. This problem has been referred to as the area of "low demand" (Lowe, 2004). The programmes used different subsidy schemes on both the supply and demand side, and both rental and low-cost ownership solutions. (This study will review the different techniques.)

Recently, there is a clear trend towards connecting these housing programmes with other social programmes in education, health care and employment. Social scientists and policy makers realised that housing programmes alone could not solve social problems. One of the conclusions arrived at through the experience of housing programmes that focused on clearing up slum areas was that, without creating a certain level of social mix, poverty and poor housing conditions are reproduced. The new area-based interventions explicitly include programme elements intervening in local economic, social and cultural processes (OECD, 1996).

Social housing problems are inter-related with housing finance. In the absence of an efficient housing finance system, most of the owner-occupied sector will be unaffordable. Even middle-income households (typically householders in the public sector, such as teachers) will have difficulty financing housing; hence, in some countries programmes have been launched to respond specifically to the needs of these groups.

## 2.3.    Governance of social housing

In our overview of housing, we are focusing on descriptions of different methods to assist vulnerable groups. However, the real significance of the different methods cannot be understood without the institutional background of national housing systems, namely the governance of housing. According to the definition by the European Social Housing Observatory CECODHAS, "social housing is housing where the access is controlled by the existence of allocation rules favouring households that have difficulties in finding accommodation in the market" (UNECE, 2003). The governance of social housing deals with the question of which institutions play a role in financing, developing, allocating and managing social housing.

In the developed countries, there is a wide range of different social housing "regimes" (Gibb, 2002; Oxley, 2000; Priemus and Boelhouwer, 1999; Priemus and Dieleman, 1999). The institutional structure of social housing is changing in the European Community. For example, housing associations in the Netherlands have become more independent from the central and local governments since the 1990s (Priemus, 2004). The same process occurred in Norway (Pedersen, 2002) and Denmark (Enberg, 2000).[4]

---

4. Beyond this issue, it is very important which ministry is responsible for housing policy.

# 3. Housing policy instruments improving access to housing of vulnerable social groups

## 3.1. Definition of vulnerable groups

The housing policies which facilitate access to housing for vulnerable social groups are the main theme of this report. The definition of those vulnerable groups should be the starting point of the report; however, we cannot find a general and "context-free" definition of these groups. Vulnerable social groups include immigrants, disabled people, the frail and elderly, Roma/Gypsy people, one-head households, the unemployed, victims of disasters and wars, and so on. The definition of vulnerable groups has a contextual and historical element, which makes the application and adaptation of any general programmes difficult.

According to the European Federation of National Organisations Working with the Homeless (FEANTSA) approach, vulnerable social groups from the point of view of housing can be defined in the context of the homelessness problem (see Appendix 7.1). This definition aims to monitor the trends and evaluate the risk of becoming homeless, and not just to count the number of homeless people (the most obvious sector of the vulnerable group). There is a narrow definition (roofless and houseless) and a wider definition – including every housing situation that could be considered inadequate in the legal, social and "physical" sense.

While homelessness is one of the most critical housing problems in developed countries, housing problems of vulnerable social groups cannot be viewed exclusively from this perspective. The key element of homelessness is the lack of the integration into society (social interaction, the labour market etc.). Insecure, inadequate and unaffordable housing are much wider terms, which relate to the institutional, economic and social settings of the society. These concepts are historical and context-related. The definitions of "inadequate" and "insecure" housing varies from country to country – and even within one country over time – and seems to be largely dependent on the given housing market.

The protection of the existing tenants' security is an extremely important aspect of an efficient housing policy, especially in transition countries. The position of tenants in transition countries is changing, as a result of altered social systems, privatisation of former public housing funds and amended housing legislation. Numerous individuals or families who did not succeed in acquiring ownership of their flats before and after the transition are now faced with problems such as unreasonable rent increases (in Slovenia about 80,000 tenant families have been faced with a more than 650 per cent increase in non-profit rents in the last 10 years); regulation is being abandoned (in Poland four to five million – mostly elderly – people living in rented flats are endangered); weaker legal protection where tenancy permanence is threatened (for example, the case of several thousand tenant families in Croatia); abandonment of any regulation or legal certainty of tenants (in Serbia and Montenegro, for example, where more than 80,000 tenant families live in flats without any rental contract or legal certainty). According to IUT estimation, it is a question of several million Europeans whose future right to adequate housing is endangered and are threatened with loss of adequate housing or even homelessness.

The working definitions of vulnerable groups with housing problems are (according to FEANTSA):

- persons without adequate[5] housing – the roofless and the houseless;

- persons whose housing position is endangered – the insecurely and inadequately housed, including:

    - tenants without legal protection (no rental contracts or efficient legal protection)

    - tenants with a legally uncertain housing position (they hold a rental contract and/or have a certain legal protection yet the legislation and/or court practice do not secure adequate legal certainty for permanent enjoyment of the accommodation or encroach on it)

    - persons endangered in their housing position due to economic status:

        • poor owners – individuals and families that own a flat but are unable to pay the operating costs

        • tenants that have insufficient means to pay the rent and operating costs

- unaffordable housing (for example key workers).

Different housing programmes have different explicit or implicit target groups, which can be described according to the above categories.

---

5. As highlighted above, there can be numerous differences among countries with respect to the definition of adequacy in housing. The picture becomes even more complex if we differentiate based on the fact whether the given housing is new or existing housing. Nevertheless, in order to ensure a minimum standard housing for all, countries should work on this issue.

## 3.2. Obstacles to housing of vulnerable groups

Housing problems for vulnerable groups related to:

- the economic system (unemployment),

- welfare regimes (safety net issues),

- housing regimes (legal and institutional framework),

- social factors (discrimination, etc.).

The role of the economic system is clearly a key factor influencing housing hardship. Not only do the level of the GDP and economic trends (like recession) have an effect on the housing system (for example, housing investment, housing availability), but the development of the economic system has significance in its own right too. The transition from a centrally planned economy towards a market economy could be a major cause of housing problems.

Different welfare regimes in Europe have different priorities in terms of helping vulnerable social groups through the social safety net and social institutions (homes for the elderly, child care, etc.). The consequences for housing of welfare regimes are important because a poor safety net increases the probability of housing problems (inadequate and insecure housing).

Housing regimes are a major factor behind the difficult housing situation for vulnerable groups, but their effects should be interpreted in the context of the existing economic and welfare regimes. In a rich country with modest income differences and a developed social care system, the ways in which housing policy deal with housing hardship are much more manageable, than in a poor country with high income differences and no safety net. Nevertheless, it can be still problematic.

In transition countries, changes to the legal system could be a risk factor in their own right. The reasons for an insecure individual housing position – according to the Slovenian experience – can be classified in accordance with the following criteria: 1. with regard to the source of the reason: the reason stems from the sphere of the state or from the sphere of an individual; 2. with regard to the nature of reason: the reason can be legal or economic. This is summarised in the following table:

| Nature | Source | |
|---|---|---|
| | Reason stems from the sphere of the state | Reason stems from the sphere of individual |
| Legal reasons | 1. Abandoning legal regulation of the tenancy sector with regard to permanence and firmness of tenancy (passivity of the state in regulating the tenancy sector).<br><br>2. Changing the legislation to the detriment of tenants, with regard to permanence and firmness of tenancy (active involvement of the state to the detriment of tenants). | No reasons can be seen |
| Economic reasons | 1. No legal regulation of rents (passivity of the state in tenancy policy).<br><br>2. Existing rent regulation is changing to the detriment of tenants (active involvement of the state to the detriment of tenants). | Poor economic and social status of tenants means they are unable to pay the rent |

Social and institutional factors may play an important role in explaining the housing problems of vulnerable groups. The discrimination against special vulnerable groups (like Roma) on the housing market could lead to serious housing problems (like social ghettos). The prejudiced behaviour of social landlords (local government or professional housing corporations) could contribute to the housing problems of vulnerable groups.

Housing policies that aim to improve access to housing for vulnerable groups have to be based on analyses of the nature of the housing hardship. It is important to understand the relative roles of the factors listed above.

### 3.3. General framework of policy instruments

Housing policy targeted to vulnerable groups has to be analysed as a complex set of policy factors which work in a specific economic, institutional and social environment. After defining the nature of the housing problem for vulnerable social groups and the factors explaining it, we can analyse the housing policy tools. The success of any housing programmes depends on how much the policy makers who designed the programme understood about the inter-relation of the different parts of the housing sector. The context of each programme is crucial. For example, if the housing finance system is not developed, housing affordability will be a problem, not only for the low-income group, but for middle-income groups as well. Thus, the social pressure for the subsidised programme will be much lower where a well-developed housing finance system is in place.

However, before presenting the elements of the programme, we will give an overview of the housing policy instruments used mainly (but not exclusively) in developed countries[6] to help vulnerable groups. The report will structure the programmes in the following way: firstly we study the policy instruments that increase the supply of decent and affordable housing. Secondly, we consider the housing finance elements, that facilitate access to housing for vulnerable groups. Finally we study the housing allowance programme. These are topics of particular importance for the transition countries, which are in the process of forming new housing policies. (In a separate point, we will give an overview of the programmes in the East-European transition countries.)

The focus of this part of the study will be on housing policy instruments, which will be structured under three headings. The supply-side subsidies aim at increasing the availability of decent and affordable housing units for vulnerable groups, through new construction and rehabilitation. The direct beneficiaries of the subsidy programmes are the public and private institutions offering housing opportunities for households. We will cover both programmes that promote rental units and those that promote owner-occupied units.

The demand-side subsidies will be discussed under two headings. Firstly, there are programmes that aim at increasing affordability for the low-income homebuyer, which can be described as demand-side subsidies for owner occupation. Secondly, there are programmes that aim at increasing affordability for tenants, which can be termed as demand-side subsidies for tenants (housing allowance programmes). We believe this grouping is appropriate to the diverse nature of housing stock and the variety of market mechanisms that have an impact on different tenure types.

---

6. The study covers mostly EU countries, but takes examples from the US, Canada, Australia and New Zealand as well. A separate chapter gives an overview of the developments in the transition countries.

These categories are not clear-cut. Certain programmes overlap the areas defined above. For example, the interest rate subsidy for low-income self-help builders can be labelled as a supply-side subsidy, or as a demand-side subsidy (for owner occupation). The other issue is that programmes tend to use more than one instrument. For example, social housing programmes typically use housing allowances, and, at the same time, can enjoy the advantages of state guarantee schemes or interest rate subsidies.

In a separate chapter, the report deals with the development of social housing in the transition countries in Eastern Europe – where after ten to fifteen years of the restructuring process, the need for social housing policy has emerged.

The aim of the study is to map the housing programme instruments used to support housing for vulnerable social groups, and to describe the most important characteristics of these techniques. We aim to be very careful in evaluating the programmes, because the effects of a particular housing policy instrument depend very much on the context (cultural, political, economic, etc.). There are several good comparative studies (Maclennan et al., 1997; Turner and Whitehead, 2002; Balchin, 1996; Doling, 1997; Donner, 2000) and at least one good example of a comprehensive evaluation of a total housing system – the evaluation of the Finnish housing finance and support systems by international experts (Ministry of the Environment, 2002). However, it is extremely difficult to evaluate different housing programmes, because (i) housing subsidy programmes operate alongside other income benefit programmes; (ii) subsidy programmes are complex (including different tax allowances and indirect off-budget subsidies); (iii) the institutional and legal background of housing markets are different (tenure structure, cost structure, legal environment, etc.).

In the comparative literature, this is one of the most difficult obstacles to understanding and comparing the effects of the same instruments in different environments. The housing policy debates in the transition counties are full of misinterpretations of "best practices" based on implementing housing policy measures and instruments that might work in a more developed environment, but cannot work in less developed countries.

The report is based on the vast literature available on housing policies, from sources including the Internet, journals and conference papers. The list of references is given in Appendix 7.4.

## 3.4.    Supply of affordable housing (supply-side subsidies)

The supply of affordable housing can be divided into two types. The first type is when the direct beneficiary of the programme is a "social" landlord who offers accommodation at a below-market price. The "government of social housing" varies widely between countries (Gibb, 2002). "Social landlords" have to follow procedures and guidelines for the allocation of public housing, defined by the housing policy in return for subsidies. The efficiency of the programmes depends very much on the degree to which social landlords can be involved or forced to follow the guidelines.

Most of the countries have a waiting list for social housing. The question is who manages and controls the allocation from the waiting list. In Denmark, the law regulates the allocation of housing units in the social sector. There is an internal waiting list (for the existing tenants of the housing associations) and an external one (for the newcomers into the sector), which are administered by the housing administration. Local authorities are entitled to dispose of every fourth vacant social housing apartment in a municipality to make sure that municipalities have access-ible housing available for persons with housing needs. Not all munici-palities use this right; often a voluntary agreement exists between the housing association and the municipality, in which vacancies are allocated to the social administration of the municipality on an ad hoc basis (Enberg, 2000). In the United Kingdom, the Housing Corporation co-ordinates the allocation policies of housing associations.

The second type of affordable housing is "low-cost" housing offered by private developers to low-income households at a below-market price. These programmes suppose that the developers have access to subsidies, which provide incentives (and potential) to increase the supply of afford-able housing. Social targeting is a crucial issue in these programmes and depends very much on the financial design and management of the programme.

There are different subsidy programmes supporting the supply of afford-able housing, including cash subsidies, tax expenditures, tax allowance, accelerated write-off, land subsidies, interest rate subsidies, guarantees, building regulations, planning and zoning (Gibb, 1996). In the 1960s and the 1970s, direct government help (e.g. cash grants or public loans) dominated the programmes, while in the 1990s there has been a shift towards indirect programmes (for example the "guarantee fund" in the Netherlands).

Relaxing the rent control is a special way to incentivise the private sector to increase rental housing,[7] and market rents may also be lowered – in certain markets over time – with the appearance of more investors (and thus larger supply).

### 3.4.1. Capital grants on the supply side

Capital grants are typical of subsidies in the public sector. The local governments' capital investments are partly capital grants from the central budget. Municipal governments in the United Kingdom have received capital grants for their investments, but more resources are used for supporting housing associations and for housing allowances. In the United States, the support of public housing has been cut back, but even today there are capital grant programmes, especially to support urban renewal programmes.

The "Hope VI" programme provided federal money for revitalising the worst of public housing. It has made grants to housing authorities in 26 states, ranging from just over US$1 million in Helena, Montana, to US$50 million for the redevelopment of Chicago's Cabrini Green. The Congress passed legislation in 1996, creating a viability test for all large public-housing projects where more than 10% of homes are empty. The law requires public housing authorities to decide whether improving such projects is cheaper than simply giving residents vouchers to find private housing. If not, they are "removed from the public-housing inventory". Chicago Housing Authority had a plan to demolish 11,000 public housing units, and to improve existing housing and build new mixed income developments. Half of the new apartments will be private housing, 20% "affordable housing" (for families with between 80% and 100% of the median income) and 30% homes for those poor enough to qualify for full public housing help (*The Economist*, 9 July 1998).

In countries where public housing is provided by public corporations (e.g. Australia and New Zealand) one of the important sources of housing investment is the state budget. However, more frequently, public housing

---

7. Rent control was widely used after the First World War, to protect tenants against rent increases justified by inflation. As a consequence of freezing the rent, private investment into the rental sector halted. Until the end of the 1960s, public housing policy focused on supporting housing supply in the public sector (municipal and co-operative), while the private rental sector was under rent control. (The private rental sector in Germany was different, as a soft rent control was used from the beginning.) Since the 1970s there has been a change in housing policy: the role of the private rental sector in housing policy has been re-thought. Abolishing rent control was one of the conditions of the revival of the private rental sector (Lind, 1999).

utilises private finance, where the government subsidises the interest or gives implicit or explicit guarantees.

The capital grant is more important to the non-governmental agencies or private developers who invest in affordable housing. Nevertheless, the system of capital grants to NGOs exists with other subsidies (like housing allowances). Its role is very significant in the United Kingdom, but rent-controlled housing (HLM) companies utilise it in France (Taffin, 2003), Canada, Finland, etc., as well. In many countries, capital grant programmes are linked to rent allowance programmes on the basis that subsidised construction loans are given only where affordable or low-income housing is included in the development. In the United States, for example, subsidised builders have to provide a certain percentage of units, which yield rents below a government-imposed ceiling, although this is only for a limited time (usually 20 years) after which it can be rented out at the market rate. Capital grants are very important in inner city projects, where the beneficiaries of the programme have to give guarantees that they will offer affordable housing for low-income households.

A well-known example of the cash capital grant subsidy on the supply side is the Housing Association Grant (HAG) – one of the most important subsidies in the British system. Since 1974, the HAG has been the main subsidy programme of government-funded housing associations, through the Housing Corporation and local authorities (Gibb, 1996; 2002). The housing association provides "low-cost housing", because the rent is limited. The tenants are appointed from the waiting list of the local governments. The rent level is partly a function of the site of the HAG, which can be compensated by the housing benefit programme. (The majority of the tenants get housing benefits.) The HAG has been changed in the last two decades. In the beginning, HAG financed between 80% and 90% of the capital cost of the investment, and it gradually decreased to 70% (in the 1970s) and to between 50% and 60% by the end of the 1990s. The Housing Corporation works in Britain as a regulator of the social landlords, which, at the same time, gives an implicit guarantee for lenders as well (Crook, et al., 1996).

The revival of the private rental sector in the UK has been an important housing policy issue since the 1980s. Different programmes were introduced; some of which used the capital grants scheme.

> "In Scotland, the government, through its housing agency, Scottish Homes, has developed a system of Grants for Renting and Owning (GRO grants) which subsidise private development and building costs on approved schemes. Several million pounds devoted to this

programme have been spent on private owner-occupied housing, built on large public housing estates at affordable prices. By doing so, owner occupation is encouraged in previously uniform areas, injecting housing tenure and income mix into them. These supply subsidies have the potential to attract direct investment into otherwise unprofitable but socially worthwhile programmes, which in turn improve housing market performance" (Gibb, 1996, pp. 171-2).

In Finland, the government's housing agency (ARA) gives capital grants among other subsidies.

"The Central Government of Finland, through its housing agency (ARA), allocates funding to municipalities for the construction of new social rental units. The ARA assistance is designed to reduce the effective project financing costs, declines in value per unit over time but the supply of units is provided at reduced rent levels. ARA offers both direct subsidised financing (called ARAVA housing) and subsidisation of privately financed loans. In addition to serving housing affordability, ARA also leads the country's housing standards through its extensive quality controls and attention to effective design and land-use. Over the years, ARA has accumulated a 372 221-unit portfolio. At present, ARA social rental housing subsidies are provided without Government appropriation, as ARA has autonomous access to funds. ARA was provided with a portfolio of loans by the Government of Finland, without the matching funding liabilities. This endowment of ARA, together with ARA's borrowing activities, enables it to assist a portfolio social rental projects on an on-going basis and provides the funds needed to assist new projects" (Asselin et al., 2002).

### 3.4.2. Tax credit to support the supply of affordable housing

Tax allowances for social housing have always been general financial incentives. The housing co-operative movement in the first half of the last century was based on special tax advantages. A variety of different tax advantages exist to support social landlords or private developers in the provision of affordable housing. For example, in Canada, the federal government provides a partial rebate of VAT on building costs for affordable rental housing. The rebate is reduced as the capital cost of the unit increases. Generally, the 7% VAT is reduced to 4.5% (European Bank for Reconstruction and Development [EBRD], 2002).

In the United States, an accelerated depreciation of rental properties was used to support the supply of rental housing, but its efficiency was questioned, as it contributed more to lowering the effective tax rates for high-income earners than to providing a stable, long-term supply of affordable housing (Gibb, 1996).

In the United Kingdom, significant tax allowances were offered through the Business Expansion Scheme (BES) between 1989 and 1993, which allowed accelerated tax write-off for individual investors (the working life of the subsidies was five years).[8] The BES gave incentives for individuals to invest in new business (among them rental housing) by giving investors up-front tax relief for investing in companies letting residential properties on assured tenancies, as long as the shares were retained for five years. The scheme was only given a five-year life (ending in 1993), although many of the BES portfolios continue to be held by investors.

The Low income Housing Tax Credit (LIHTC) in the United States has been the major federal programme for producing affordable rental housing since its creation as part of the Tax Reform Act (TRA) of 1986. It is an alternative method of funding housing for low and moderate income households, and has been in operation since 1987.[9] The LIHTC represents a partnership between a variety of public and private sector parties. Until 2000, each state received a tax credit of US$1.25 per person, which it can allocate towards funding housing that meets programme guidelines (currently, legislation is pending to increase this per capita allocation). This per capita allocation was raised to US$1.50 in 2001, and to US$1.75 in 2002, and from the beginning of 2003 it has been adjusted to reflect inflation. These tax credits are then used to leverage private capital into new construction, or acquisition and rehabilitation of affordable housing.

The basic premise of the LIHTC is to offer federal tax credits to private investors in return for their providing equity for the development of affordable rental housing. The programme is administered by state (or, in a few cases, local) housing policy makers, who set goals for the programme, review projects proposed by for-profit and not-for-profit developers, monitor the reasonableness of project costs, and take responsibility for ensuring that projects stay in compliance and that approved projects receive only the tax credits necessary to make the project work.

---

8. Earlier, in 1982, another scheme was used. Eligible landlords providing assured tenancy could deduct 75% of the cost of construction of dwellings to be let on assured tenancies from income in the first year, followed by 4% per annum thereafter (Holmans et al., 2002).

9. In the United States, raising capital for affordable housing was supported through tax-exempt bond issues, backed by project revenues. State Housing Finance Agencies provided institutional infrastructure to underwrite and issue tax-exempt bonds (Pomeroy, 2004).

Tax Credits must be used for new construction, rehabilitation, or acquisition and rehabilitation, and projects must also meet the following requirements: 20% or more of the residential units in the project are both rent restricted and occupied by individuals whose income is 50% or less of the median gross income in the area, or if 40% or more of the residential units in the project are both rent restricted and occupied by individuals whose income is 60 percent or less of the median gross income in the area. When the LIHTC programme began in 1987, properties receiving tax credits were required to stay eligible for 15 years. This eligibility time period has since been increased to 30 years. The Internal Revenue Service (IRS) is responsible for monitoring compliance and state performance (Cummings and Denise DiPasquale, 1999; Green and Malpezzi, 2003).

### 3.4.3. Techniques to enhance mixed neighbourhood formation

In the United States, inclusionary zoning[10] is one planning technique which supports the supply of affordable housing. At local level, this aim is attained through a zoning ordinance, with objectives for the inclusion of the below-market housing in the area of housing development. The ordinance requires builders to include a certain amount of housing for low and moderate income households. In summary, inclusionary zoning has been criticised for shifting the burden of affordable housing provision to other groups, for distilling the upwardly mobile poor from the remainder of central city residents and for causing undue growth in locations that would not otherwise experience it (Burchell and Galley, 2000).

In Los Angeles a proposal was put forward that would require housing developers to offer below-market units in the city. Developers of five or more rental units would be required to set aside 12% of the units in their projects for low-income households and 10% of the units for participants in the housing voucher programme (Section 8). Developers of five or more condominiums and single family houses would have to earmark 20% to 40% of the units for below-market buyers (*Los Angeles Times*, 10 August 2004).

In the United Kingdom, under Section 106 of the Town and Country Planning Act, the local council and developers have to make a contract that includes conditions for the provision of "affordable housing". It seems

---

10. In contrast, exclusionary zoning is a technique that effectively drives up the cost of housing, excluding lower income households from the community. Exclusionary zoning practices have been under attack in communities around the United States for decades, most notably in New Jersey, where the historic Mount Laurel decisions have led the way in promoting inclusionary zoning techniques and creating affordable housing (http://www.inhousing.org).

to be very similar to inclusionary zoning in the United States, but leaves more room for negotiation, as the contract has to be made case by case. The Mayor of London, Ken Livingstone, has issued a draft supplementary planning guidance on his target that 50% of new homes in London should be affordable.

In other countries, local governments use planning rights to bargain for more affordable housing. In the urban renewal programmes, special planning negotiations can help to provide more affordable housing.

The governments' affordable housing policy is realised in several countries through land policy. Selling land at below-market price for development is frequently used in exchange for "affordable housing" programmes. In order for this to benefit the end consumer there has to be some price control for the housing, to prevent the subsidy from ending up among the producers.

### 3.4.4. Interest rate subsidies

Interest rate subsidy programmes can be managed through public institutions or through private financial institutions. The difference is that through public institutions other hidden subsidies can be involved, too. The programme can make use of different funds (such as pension funds, social security funds, special wage taxes, or even the budget resources). In both cases, the government programme reduces the interest rate paid by the social landlord or the developer.

*French HLM special interest rate subsidy.* Another feature of the social housing sector is the involvement of specialist operators – the social housing bodies – of which there are more than 1 200. Three quarters of these are moderate rent housing agencies or *organismes d'habitations a loyer modéré* (HLM) and one quarter are *sociétés d'économie mixte à activité immobilière* (semi-public property companies). The HLM agencies can be public or private bodies, depending on whether they are public limited companies, co-operative societies or local public corporations. These agencies enjoy a number of advantages and are subject to certain statutory duties. To build social housing, the agencies use a cheap long-term loan: the *prêt locatif à usage social* (PLUS) loan for building low-cost housing, with an interest rate which stood at 3.45% in 2000. The loan is financed from the deposits savers put into their National Savings Bank (Caisse d'Épargne) or France's most popular savings account, the French Post Office's "Livret A". These deposits are managed by a special state-owned financial institution, the *Caisse des dépôts et consignations* [official deposits, investments, savings management, etc.]. The agencies also benefit from a state subsidy, at a rate which varies between 5% and 12% (and on occasion as high as 25%) depending on the operation.[11]

### 3.4.5. Guarantees and insurance

Social housing organised through the municipal sector typically enjoys state guarantees for long-term private sector loans. In the co-operative sector, these guarantees were generally assured (as in Denmark, for example). In the 1990s, public housing was financed more and more by the private sector. A range of mortgage guarantee schemes was available to assist the private sector finance. In the United Kingdom, the Housing Corporation has a regulatory oversight over the registered social landlords, and extensive powers, including the ability to replace the board members and the manager of the housing association (EBRD, 2002).

> "Prior to 1978 all social housing in Canada was financed directly by the federal government through its housing agency Canada Mortgage and Housing Corporation (CMHC), sometimes in partnership with the provincial housing agencies. In 1978 there was a major policy shift to 100% private financing, in part to address issues of excess cash demands on the federal treasury. Private lending was encouraged and facilitated by: the use of CMHC mortgage insurance to cover 100% of loss in case of default; and an ongoing 35-year subsidy commitment that provided cash flow to ensure mortgage repayment. Together, this provided a double guarantee on loans backed by federal government, so minimal risk. Meanwhile, loans were fairly attractive to lenders, with no prepayment options (so eliminating prepayment risk) and interest rates set at midpoint of market range for that term (usually renewable five year terms, amortised over 35 yrs). The new approach effectively engaged the private sector; especially as mortgage intermediaries (brokers) aggressively marketed the social housing product to institutional investors. But private financing was not necessarily cost effective, since rates at mid-point of range for retail mortgages were high relative to risk (given the two forms of government backing)" (Pomeroy, 2004).

In the Netherlands, the restructuring process of the public housing sector shows the significance of mortgage insurance in the supply of affordable housing.

As a consequence of the budget constraints on social housing a guarantee fund was introduced in the mid 1980s to cover the risk of loans for

---

11. http://www.environment.fi/default.asp?node=10794&lan=en#a2.

renovation of social housing.[12] Since 1990, this initiative has been extended to cover loans for new houses and has replaced state and municipal guarantees on old loans. Parallel to the introduction of the Guarantee Fund Social Housing, the financial system was completely restructured. All state obligations to the social housing sector were capitalised via the net present value method (i.e. subsidies on operating deficit) as well as the financial obligations of the housing associations. The debts were settled in one major operation, whereby the direct financial ties between housing associations and the state were dissolved. From that moment, the social housing sector itself became responsible for the (financially) sound operation of their stock. In practice, this is possible because realised profits from some of the stock can be used to cover deficits in others. Rent increases are still subject to political decisions, but a system has been adopted which settles an average rent increase (a few points) above the level of inflation. Housing associations are free to implement diversified rent increases for their housing projects within the limits of the average rent increase and the maximum fair rent appropriate to the quality of the project. Subsidies for operating deficits do not exist. A specific security structure has been established to facilitate the financing of the Dutch social rental sector. This structure virtually eliminates credit and default risks for the investor. Because of the security structure, default risk is not associated with individual housing associations, but with the whole of the social rental sector and the Dutch state. Housing associations are responsible for ensuring their own financial continuity. Rental income, financial income and asset value need to be adequate in this respect. However, should a housing association expect to make a loss, then the Dutch Central Fund for Social Housing can provide financial support. The Dutch Central Fund for Social Housing is a public body, which acts on behalf of the Dutch Minister of Social Housing. It has responsibility for monitoring the financial position of housing associations, both individually and collectively. The Dutch Central Fund for Social Housing imposes levies on all housing associations, making it compulsory to generate financial means for this support. Support may be provided in the form of interest-free subordinated loans to individual housing associations. The Dutch Central Fund for Social Housing can grant financial support, possibly combined with a restructuring. Restructuring can be enforced by the Minister of Social Housing on the initiative of the Dutch Central Fund for Social Housing. As additional security for lending institutions and investors, the Guarantee Fund can provide guarantees. Guarantees cover the total debt service and are provided for borrowing relating to

12. This summary is based on Elbers, 2003.

identified property only. The Guarantee Fund has its capital invested in sound financial assets, which can be immediately converted into cash if necessary. Additional capital can and will be demanded by the Guarantee Fund from participants, if the fund's capital becomes less than 0.25% of the total guaranteed capital. These recoverable monies consist of a fixed percentage of 2.5% or 3.75% respectively, of the original nominal amount borrowed. The ultimate security to lending institutions and investors is the joint and unlimited backstop agreements between the central government, the municipalities and the Guarantee Fund. If – once the limited recoverable receivables due by participants have been demanded and collected – the capital of the Guarantee Fund would still be lower than 0.25% of the total guaranteed capital, then the central Government and municipalities will provide interest-free loans to the Guarantee Fund to meet this capital requirement and allow them to fulfil any guarantee obligations.

### 3.5. Access to housing finance (demand-side subsidies for owner occupation)

Low-income households' access to home ownership is constrained by several factors. Firstly, low-income households struggle to join the owner-occupied sector, because they do not have access to the minimum amount of savings to make a downpayment, and because they do not have access to long-term mortgages. Typical demand-side subsidies (for owner occupation) aim to assist households who are on the margins of affordability, into owner occupation. In principle, the social housing sector has to provide accommodation for the poorest households, but the size of the social sector is limited in most of the countries, and there is a declining tendency (Harloe, 1995).

The rationale behind the low-income home ownership subsidy programmes is that a household precluded from the social sector can have access to low-cost homes through a modest contribution of their own. In principle, these households should be better off than households in the social sector, but in reality this is not necessarily the case. Low-cost home ownership programmes are supported by the shift in housing policy which supposes that home ownership represents a superior tenure to social rental (Bramley and Morgan, 1998). The other justification for the low-cost home ownership programme is to encourage a social mix in neighbourhoods.

Two models have been applied for targeting subsidies in order to achieve either direct or indirect help for low-income households. Whereas one emphasises concrete and specific actions, targeted to the lower strata of society, the latter relies on the trickle-down or filtering effects. The filtering down effect pre-supposes that when the upper part of the market is subsidised, there will be vacant housing at the lower part of the market for low-income households. Filtering down subsidies might be effective in housing markets where the supply is differentiated by quality, size and cost and where there is no general shortage of housing. There are different grant schemes to support low-income group access to homeownership. These are basically demand-side subsidies, which increase the purchasing power of households, improving affordability. There are several grant strategies or grant design methods, depending on which financial element is supported. Firstly, there are programmes that try to help to fulfil the cash downpayment requirement of home buying. A typical example is the demand-side capital grant used in countries like Chile, South Africa and Hungary. Self-help housing is also an option, providing easier access to housing and improvement in housing quality for low-income groups – as was applied in Sweden and Norway when they were experiencing severe housing shortages. This solution seems most reasonable in countries with a housing shortage. Another interesting solution is the shared ownership schemes (used in Britain and Ireland) that decrease the total price of homes bought by the eligible households. There are subsidy programmes which incentivise households to save for housing, making it easier for them to make the cash downpayment. The loan/value ratio for low-income groups can be increased by taking over a part or the total risk of mortgages, through public banks or public insurance/guarantee schemes. The loan/value ratio can also be increased through interest rate and tax allowances.

### 3.5.1.   Capital grants, cash subsidy

Capital grants provided directly to households are relatively rare in EU countries. The reason is that a relatively large social sector means that households who apply for low-cost housing may already have some savings, and could afford a loan (typically with preferential interest rate, tax advantages, guaranteed higher loan-to-value ratio and so on). Nevertheless, in countries where the social sector is underdeveloped, and the housing finance system is "immature",[13] cash subsidies could be very efficient. In transition countries, after the regime change, the situation was in several respects similar to that of the developing countries. Therefore, it is reasonable to consider the experiences of direct demand subsidy schemes in South America. The first direct demand subsidy programme was introduced in Chile in 1974, but in the 1980s and 1990s other countries also

---

13. For example, high collateral is expected, low loan-to-value ratio, etc.

introduced direct grant subsidy programmes (Ferguson and Navarrete, 2003; Ferguson, Rubinstein and Dominguez, 1996; Conway and Mikelsons, 1996).

Direct demand grants typically replaced the below-market interest rate mortgage finance programmes and proved to be much more efficient in terms of targeting, transparency and predictability. In an uncertain financial environment, the interest rate subsidies might involve a huge fiscal risk for governments, depending on the structure and design of the interest rate subsidy scheme (this was one of the reasons for the radical change to the subsidy scheme in Hungary in 2004).

The designs of direct subsidy programmes vary greatly, and some critics have suggested that, in several cases, the beneficiaries were middle-income groups. In Chile, for example, the allocation of the grant (Ferguson, Rubinstein and Dominguez, 1996) was based on a score system that included factors related to needs (housing situation, income, etc.) and the households' efforts to save. Naturally, the capacity to save excludes the poorest groups from the programme. Eligible households receive the subsidy in the form of vouchers, which could be used to fund new construction or to purchase existing housing.

The rationale behind the programme was that needy households could finance their housing with their own savings, a downpayment subsidy or a market-rate mortgage. For different income groups, diverse subsidy schemes were defined. (Higher-income households were expected to save more, and have fewer subsidies.)

The institutional background was an interesting and important element of these programmes: the private and non-governmental sector played a crucial role in the allocation of the grant and in the programme execution, which influenced the efficiency of the use of the grant. The programme in Costa Rica was the most successful in reaching the poorest target group, because "NGOs experienced in housing development and in working with low-income groups have become the main developers under the programme, rather than the profit developers" (Ferguson, Rubinstein and Dominguez, 1996).

In Ecuador, a cash subsidy replaced the interest rate subsidy programme in 1998 and proved to be more efficient. Households who can demonstrate they have savings are eligible for a "voucher" (cash grant) to buy or to renew a home. The voucher for renewal is US$750 (US$850 for the city centre). The household can take a local market loan to bridge the gap between the cost and their resources (savings and grant) (Frank, 2004).

One of the examples of the cash subsidy programme in Europe is the Grants for Renting and Owning programme by Scottish Homes, which gives households a direct cash grant to build or renovate property, typically in the special rehabilitation areas (Gibb, 1996; Bramley and Morgan, 1998).

A cash subsidy for special programmes exists in Norway as well. First home grants help especially disadvantaged households to establish themselves and to maintain an acceptable home, mainly in rental housing.

### 3.5.2. Shared ownership, equity loan

In Britain (and Ireland), shared ownership programmes are used to enable low-income households to buy homes that have a higher price than they could otherwise afford. The householder purchases an affordable portion of the value of the home, and rents the remaining portion from a social landlord (typically these programmes are run by housing associations). Shared ownership schemes are aimed at people who cannot afford to buy their home in one go. It allows eligible householders to buy a proportion of the home to begin with, increasing that proportion step by step until they own the whole house. Until then, ownership is shared between them and the institution that manages the programme (the local authority, or a social landlord, such as a housing association). Householders make payments on a mortgage for the part they own and pay rent for the other part.

Eligibility criteria are established by the social landlord for the shared ownership scheme. Again, targeting is an important part of the programme; households have to meet the criteria set by the landlord or local authority. Social landlords not only offer their own new or existing homes, but also allow applicants to find homes on the open market. Nevertheless, these homes must meet certain minimum standards and be suitable for the household's needs – they also have to be approved by the local authority.

There are different versions of shared ownership depending on the legal structure of the contracts. "Sharing owners are long leaseholders (in England and Wales) or have an occupancy agreement (Scotland) and are responsible for all maintenance" (Bramley and Morgan, 1998).

"Equity loan" (Homebuy) is another type of low-cost shared ownership programme in Britain. Under this scheme the eligible household gets an interest-free loan equivalent to 25% (formerly 30%) of the property value, and pays for the remaining part. The social landlord covers the cost of the loan (there is no rent payable by the household).

Successful shared ownership depends on an appropriate legal background and a well-developed practice. The British experience shows problems deriving from the complexity of the programmes (such as too many variations and unsolved conflicts in cases of repossession).

The demand for low-cost home ownership (LCHO) is very strong in high-value areas, such as Greater London. This model could be very efficient for programmes aimed at helping "key workers", because increased house prices make housing unaffordable for people with average incomes and below. This is the case in the health service and for teachers, transport workers and others on whom the success of the local economy depends (Martin, 2001).

### 3.5.3.  Contract saving systems for housing

To increase affordability, several countries support special saving schemes for housing (Dübel, 2000). These are voluntary saving products that offer some financial incentives for the savers in the form of premium, tax allowances and so on. The typical and most commonly used model is the German Bauspar system. Bausparkassen are specialised (closed) financial institutions, designed to collect savings deposits on a regular basis at a low, below-market rate and to recycle the low rate on their funding into low rates on loans for "housing purposes". The savers enjoy a premium in addition to their savings.

The French Epargne Logement system is an open system that gives incentives to savers. Home ownership savings accounts and savings plans are available to all, and enable savers to enjoy tax relief on the interest earned from these accounts and to receive a bonus from the state when they take out a loan to buy property.[14]

*Finland: ASP loans for first-time homebuyers.* The ASP savings and loan scheme is designed for young first-time homebuyers, between 18 and 30 years old. ASP agreements commit borrowers to save a certain amount as a downpayment for their first home, while the bank is committed to grant them a loan once they reach their savings target. Buyers must save 15% of the price of their home in a special ASP account. Other finances than those in the ASP account may be used towards the cost of the home, but they will not be counted as ASP savings. Initially, the bank pays a tax-free interest rate of 1% on ASP savings, but when the savings target has been reached and the purchase or construction of the home is completed, an additional tax-free interest rate of 2%-4% is paid. Interest rates on loans covered by interest subsidies are then agreed with the bank, together

---

14. www.ambafrance- uk.org/asp/service.asp?SERVID=100&LNG=en&PAGID=95.

with other repayment conditions. Banks are obliged to grant such loans at lower interest rates than those charged on loans given to other first-time home buyers. ASP loans are not conditional on factors such as borrowers' income levels. This form of housing subsidy is intended for every young first-time home buyer.[15]

In many central and eastern European economies, subsidised savings schemes of the German type have been exported to encourage saving for housing. As concluded by Lea and Renaud (1994), such systems are inappropriate for high-inflation countries, where the bulk of the subsidy is going towards offsetting inflation, and the net rewards for saving in the system – relative to saving in a bank – are very dependent on the course of inflation during the contract period. Moreover, fears that these systems could be very expensive, and that the budget burden would be politically difficult to manage, have been confirmed. The situation in the Czech Republic, where the annual bonus has been untouchable, while market interest rates have plummeted, highlights how extreme their impact can be (Dübel, 2003). Reports from Hungary and Slovakia indicate that any decline in new contracts prompts immediate pressure to boost subsidies further, confirming the expectation that the inherently unstable structure of the system distorts political decisions about what forms housing subsidies should take (Diamond, 1998). From the low-income group's perspective, the critical point is that the saving capacity of these households is very limited, preventing them from enjoying the advantages of this model.

### 3.5.4. Guarantees

The typical constraint of low-cost home ownership programmes is the reluctance of banks to take the risk related to mortgage loans given to low-income households (credit rationing problem). There are two ways to overcome this obstacle: firstly, through state-owned, public mortgages; secondly, by giving a private or public guarantee to banks issuing individual loans (Buckley et al., 2003). The main feature of these programmes is risk sharing – that is, the state provides an implicit or explicit guarantee up to a certain point (Hoek-Smit and Diamond, 2003). (The banks should bear the basic credit risk.)

For low-income groups, overcoming the credit-rationing problem can be difficult, even in developed financial systems. They would typically need to make high downpayments to potential mortgage lenders, in order to reduce their higher credit risk. To solve this problem, private banks need

---

15. www.environment.fi/default.asp?node=10794&lan=en#a2.

a guarantee to decrease the risk associated with loans given to low-income groups. Thus, the government or a government agency will give a guarantee, typically together with other subsidies. As state lending decreases, governments are increasingly applying this measure indirectly to help low-income households – who might have difficulty getting a mortgage loan – into owner occupation. Without this help, the private market will not accept the risk at rates that are affordable for vulnerable groups. State loans are then replaced by mortgage guarantees or insurance in many countries (Turner and Whitehead, 2002).

In the Netherlands, the Home Owners'Guarantee Fund, which was set up in 1993, gives special support to enable lower-income groups to have access to homeownership. The fund – also called the National Mortgage Guarantee (NMG) – is an independent foundation that provides a guarantee for loans of private house buyers. The Homeownership Guarantee Fund is a private institution, with fallback agreements with the government and municipalities. These agreements form the basis for interest-free loans received by the fund from the government and municipalities, at times when their assets are no longer sufficient. This means that the fund is able to comply with its payment obligations at all times. As a result, the Netherlands Central Bank (De Nederlandsche Bank) considers the NMG to be a government guarantee. Consequently, loans covered by the NMG are exempt from solvency requirements for the lender. The fund stands surety for the repayment of mortgage payments to the lender. If income is reduced by, for instance, unemployment, disability or divorce, the dwelling may have to be sold and may fetch less than the amount still to be repaid, resulting in a residual debt. The fund pays the residual debt to the lender. Because of this security, the lender charges a lower interest rate. The interest advantage may be as high as 0.5%. If, in the opinion of the fund, the forced sale cannot be attributed to the owner and the owner has tried to limit the residual debt as far as possible, the fund will waive the residual debt. The most important condition for the NMG is that the dwelling costs no more than €230 000, including all additional costs such as civil law notary costs, commission and refurbishment.[16]

The New Zealand government introduced a lender's mortgage insurance scheme in September 2003. The aim of the programme was to increase the lenders' willingness to extend credit to under-served markets. The target groups are young low-income households (first-time homebuyers). They are eligible to get a loan maximum 100 000 New Zealand dollars with 100% loan-to-value ratio. Borrowers receive a counselling service

16. www.nhg.nl/content/content.aspx?id=0&cid=8.

before and after the loan is taken. One of the key features of the scheme is pre- and post-purchase support to ensure that buyers are aware of what owning a home involves and that early support can be put in place if borrowers have difficulty meeting mortgage payments (Clapham and Fitzgerald, 2004).

In Finland, in the framework of the Loan Guarantee Programme, while mortgages are generally limited to 70% of the value of the property being financed, lenders will agree to raise their loan-to-value ratio to 85% in instances where ARA undertakes to protect the financial institution against a portion of their mortgage default losses. In instances where the prospective homeowner receives an interest subsidy, the loan guarantee is available at no charge; otherwise, the loan applicant can obtain the guarantee against a 2.5% guarantee premium (Asselin et al., 2002).

### 3.5.5. Interest rate subsidy

One of the most popular demand-side subsidies has been the interest rate subsidy in order to reduce the interest paid by the borrower to the landlord. There are different schemes depending on the funding structure. The government can pay a fixed amount or a portion of interest to the lender, or can provide support to the funding used for housing loans (Hoek-Smit and Diamond, 2003).

Denmark has a special procedure to support pensioners in owner-occupied houses: an allowance is given as a subsidised loan, which has to be repaid when the house is sold. The amount of the subsidy is, however, small (Turner et al., 1996).

Typically, interest rate subsidies are not means-tested programmes. However, in the US, a means-tested version – called the Down Payment/ Closing Cost Assistance Programme – exists on a limited scale. First-time home buyers wanting to purchase a new home through the Homebuyers Opportunity Programme (HOP) or a re-sale/existing home buyer can borrow up to US$5 000 at 3% interest, to be used towards the downpayment and closing costs. The loan is in the form of a second trust and is paid back over a five-year period. The loan is limited to first-time home buyers or those who have not owned a home within the last three years. Funding is limited and available on a first come, first served basis.[17]

The Norwegian implicit subsidy system is based on the fact that the Norwegian State Housing Bank does not differentiate the interest rate on mortgages by risk, as ordinary banks do. This means that low-income

---

17. www.hud.gov/.

households will get the same interest rate as high-income households. The interest rate matches the best offers in the private market. The implicit subsidy is thus the difference between the interest rate that the household would get on the private market and the Housing Bank's rate.

In Greece, interest-free loans are provided for the completion, extension or repair of existing homes. Loans are financed by the Workers' Housing Organisation, and amount to €12 000 (plus €3 000 per child) in the case of completion, and €7 500 (plus €1 000 per child) for repair. The loans have to be repaid within 15 years (in the border region: 20 years). In addition, for large families (at least four children, or at least three where one has a disability, or anybody in the family has a disability) can receive an interest-free loan to purchase or construct a house (€9 000 plus €9 000 for every child beyond the fifth). These loans are repaid over 25 years.

### 3.5.6. Tax exemptions and affordable housing

The favourable tax treatment of households in the owner-occupied sector has been a widely used technique. These subsidies (in the form of tax relief or tax credit for the mortgage repayment, tax advantages of capital gain tax for owner-occupiers, and reduced property tax or lack of the imputed tax) were – and to some extent still are – used in developed countries without means testing or any targeting. In the 1980s and 1990s, there was a general tendency to decrease these expenditures,[18] and to introduce certain targeting into the system of tax allowances (Turner et al., 1996; Scanlon and Whitehead, 2004).

The means of targeting are income ceilings for deduction, or limiting the subsidy just for first-time buyers.

In Finland the national general income tax system reduces the effective financial cost of home ownership loans by providing tax rebates (rather than deductions from taxable income) equivalent to 29% of mortgage interest costs for all home owners with a mortgage (30% for first-time home-buyers) up to a maximum level determined by the household size. First-time home buyers are also exempted from property transfer tax, which is normally 1.6% of the acquisition of homes owned by a housing company, and 4% for real estate deals. Homes may be sold tax-free after two years of ownership, until when a capital gains tax (currently set at 29%) is payable by the seller.[19]

---

18. In Germany, France and UK there is no mortgage interest relief (ECB, 2004. p. 36).
19. www.environment.fi/default.asp?node=10794&lan=en (date of downloading: May 2005).

In Germany, home ownership tax allowances were introduced in 1996 for first-time buyers, which made it possible to deduct 6% of the production or purchase price (up to a ceiling) in the first four years, and 5% in the second four years. Families with children are eligible for a higher deduction.

### 3.5.7. Housing support for home buyers[20]

There are programmes helping low-income or first-time home buyers to meet their monthly expenditure, relating to their new home. In the US, the housing voucher programme has been supplemented by an option to use the voucher for home buyers. Under Section 8, the "home ownership option" authorised the public housing agency (PHA) to provide tenant-based assistance for an eligible family that purchases a dwelling unit that will be occupied by the family. This permits the PHA to use the voucher subsidy to assist an eligible first-time home owner with their monthly home ownership expenses instead of the rent. The homeownership voucher option is a special housing type under the housing choice voucher programme. This means that PHAs may choose to offer the home ownership option as part of their housing choice voucher programmes but are not required to do so. The PHA may also choose to impose limits on the size of its voucher home ownership programme.

In the Netherlands, the national government and municipalities fulfil a safety net function in the event that the fund suffers considerable losses. In order to promote owner-occupied housing, a monthly subsidy has been available for home owners since 2001, provided conditions are met in terms of income, sales price and mortgage amount.

In the United Kingdom, well over 300 000 people are qualified to receive help from the government with their mortgage payments under a scheme known as Income Support for Mortgage Interest (ISMI).[21] Critics of the present housing benefit programmes in the United Kingdom deliver proposals to include poor home owners in the subsidy programme. Half of the poorest households live in the owner-occupied sector. Compared with low-income tenants, they are more likely to be in low-paid work or retired, and less likely to be out of work. Because low-income owner-occupiers are not eligible for Housing Benefit, they can be worse off in work than the unemployed (Kemp, Wilcox, Rhodes, 2002).

---

20. We will deal with housing allowances in the next point. Here we limit our interest to the housing support related to home buying, meaning a special demand-side subsidy to help access to owner-occupied housing.
21. www.themovechannel.com/howto/manage-money/protection-products/why-buy-ppi.asp/.

Greece also applies a special subsidy scheme for mortgage payers (only for loans to the Workers' Housing Organisation) in case they have to pay more than 20% of their monthly income for each instalment, or 10% to 15% for families with children (decisions are made on a case-by-case basis). If the family has more than four children, 50% of the debt to the organisation is written off. Special conditions can be applied for those who become unemployed after signing a contract with the housing organisation.

### 3.5.8.    Land provision – assisting self-help housing

Inclusion of informal techniques of land markets can provide a successful tool for raising housing access for vulnerable groups, as we can observe in some countries in South America and Asia. In recent years two programmes – one in Pakistan and one in the Philippines – were launched to explore the effects of "copying" black market structures in housing assistance schemes. Both programmes were based on legalising land use; all further elements diverged in the two models.

They both have some bottlenecks. The sustainability of the programme in the Philippines is questionable, due to the high costs of the interest rate subsidy. In Pakistan – because the targeting criteria were to provide access for the poorest people – an over-targeting occurred, hence the new housing area was becoming stigmatised and did not have the desirable social mix of inhabitants that is common for previously formed low-cost settlements (Berner, 2001).

### 3.5.9.    Ready-built housing for low-income households

A special type of programme is applied in Greece, where ready-to-occupy houses built by private building contractors are sold to the Workers' Housing Organisation, which allocates them, or the housing organisation itself purchases homes and appoints them to individual households. The target group is those needy households who cannot afford to take out a loan. There are thresholds of eligibility according to household composition (five or more dependants, children with disabilities, orphans, disabled pensioners). These houses are in estates planned by the housing organisation; thus, they are well equipped with infrastructure. An additional feature of the programme is that, despite the fact that the beneficiaries receive full ownership of the allocated flats, the responsibility for renovation remains that of the housing organisation.

### 3.6.   Housing allowances (demand-side subsidies)

Housing allowances are a liquidity support to low-income households, enabling them to consume more on housing than would have been possible without the support.

Housing allowances have a long tradition in Europe. In Scandinavia, housing allowances have been an integral part of housing policy since the 1940s. Most EU member states have some system of housing allowances (Belgium, Luxembourg and Portugal are exceptions).

Numerous techniques have been applied since the early 1970s throughout the European housing systems, indicating a shift from the supply-side subsidy to the demand-side subsidy. The aim of this change was to enlarge the target control (Stephens, 2004). Hence, different states applied a variety of subsidy schemes, resulting in a diversity of supported tenure types, target groups and covered household types. The evolving forms, their effects and possible measurements of effectiveness have been intensely investigated in several policy analyses (e.g. Howenstine, 1986; Priemus, 2000; Ditch et al., 2001; Fallis, 1990) and have featured as themes of scientific conferences as well (Bradshaw and Finch, 2003; Nordvik and Åhrén, 2004; Stephens 2004). The most discussed issues included the comparative effects and technical set-ups of housing allowance schemes.

The importance of housing allowances differs from country to country. In Finland and Sweden, housing allowances constitute around 50% of total support for housing (including tax subsidies) in 2002 (Åhrén, 2004). In Denmark, Finland and Sweden about 20% of households received housing allowances in 2002 (ibid.).

In contrast to these figures, we can look at the coverage of housing allowances in central and eastern European countries around 2002 to 2003. In the Czech Republic, 7.1% of households received housing allowances. The figure for Hungary is 7.3%, 7% in Poland, 3.45% in Slovakia and 0.5% in Slovenia (Hegedüs and Teller, 2005)."However, it is important to emphasise that housing allowance systems are changing, and in almost every transition country the housing allowance systems are under 'pressure'. For example, the rent regulation is under constant criticism in the Czech Republic and in Slovenia, and any change to the rent control could have a significant effect on the housing allowances" (Hegedüs and Teller, 2005).

Housing allowance is one of the most important demand-side subsidies. However, like other subsidy schemes, this has to be put in the context of the housing and welfare system of the given country. Housing allowances are embedded in the social income support system. Three types of housing allowance programmes are identified in the literature (Kemp, 1990,1997; Ditch et al., 2001; Hulse, 2002):

- social assistance, which is a part of the income benefit programmes where housing expenditures are considered among the items determining the size of the transfer;

- separate income support, which supplements the general income benefit programmes;

- housing subsidy (allowance), which is given separately from the income benefit supports.

Hulse (2002) analyses housing allowance systems in five countries[22] and concludes that housing allowances in Ontario, Canada belong to the first group (income deficit model), the Australian and New Zealand housing allowances to the second group (income supplement model), and the United States' housing voucher programme to the third group (housing assistance model).

Housing allowances are typically used to support the tenants of the rental sector, however (as in the United States), there are designs in which home owners are eligible as well.[23] In this part of the study, we will limit the overview to the issues related to housing allowances in the rental sector.

National housing allowance systems can be very different, but one of the most important dividing lines between the housing allowance systems is entitlement: namely, the interpretation of "entitlement". In most of the European countries, rent subsidy is a "right" for tenants, while in the United States, there is a waiting list from which the Public Housing Authority allocates the limited number of rent certificates (Priemus, 2000). The United States' housing voucher programme is a closed-ended programme, whereas most European countries run open-ended programmes.[24]

While a converging process can be detected in most countries, putting more and more weight on demand-side subsidies, we have to be aware

---

22. The countries represent "liberal welfare regimes" (Esping-Andersen, 1999), which can be characterised by a narrow definition of social responsibilities and promoting private market solution (Hulse, 2002).

23. In Germany, New Zealand, Sweden and France for example, home owners can receive housing allowances according to different rules.

24. However, an open-ended programme can be as limited as a generous close-ended programme.

of the emergence of diverging technical solutions to housing allowances.

### 3.6.1. Design of the formula

Housing allowance programmes differ according to the type of formula they use. In the literature two basic types of formulae can be differentiated: firstly, the gap formula and secondly the residual income formula (Kemp, 1990, 1997; Stephens and Steen, 2004). Both schemes are based on the recognition that housing costs (in most cases rent expenses) put a burden on low-income groups, which should be reduced. Nevertheless, the more prevalent gap formula (as applied in the Netherlands, for example) is founded on the acknowledgement that after a socially accepted minimum contribution to housing costs, further housing costs or a given ratio of them are paid by the state. The residual income formula (in the United Kingdom, for example) approaches the affordability issue in a different way: it sets the minimum amount a household should have at its disposal after paying all housing costs, and the state complements the beneficiaries' residual income up to this sum. Theoretically, the latter formula focuses on lower-income groups more and offers more safety net functions, whereas the first one can be distributed more evenly among the different income groups and hence has a more accentuated affordability function.

In Australia, the private sector rent assistance is a cost gap scheme. Above a minimum threshold, the allowance covers 75% of the rent, but only, however up to the level of the maximum limit. The result is a maximum coverage of 35% to 45% of the rent, depending on the composition of the household. In Canada, private sector rent assistance covers all the rent, however there are strict limits set on eligible rents. Since this varies according to the province, 65% to 70% of the market average rent is covered. In France, the variance of the rent coverage is great, since the formula takes rents, earnings and household composition into consideration. The Netherlands operates a cost gap housing allowance scheme, where the rents are grouped into three bands. The minimum band eligible rents are supported completely; the two further ones by 25% and 50%. Most households are eligible for the 75% band. Sweden applies a cost gap formula as well. There are two bands of 75% and 50% (Ditch et al., 2001).

### 3.6.2. Eligibility criteria: targeting

Housing allowance programmes differ with respect to the eligible households. In the United States and Australia, for example, only tenants in the private rental sector are eligible for housing allowance, while in the United Kingdom there are different programmes for public sector tenants and private sector tenants. In Germany, New Zealand, Sweden and France, owners are also eligible for housing allowance – however, in Germany and Ireland, the support for this target group is much more limited than in the rental sector (in Germany, 40% of the renters receive housing allowance; in Ireland 10%, less than 1% of owner households are included in the schemes). Austria's housing allowance scheme is directed at the private rental sector.

Targeting, in all cases, is based on means testing and, in some cases, additional conditions – such as family type, retired status, and vulnerability – make targeting more accurate. As housing allowance schemes are directed to diverging target groups, their coverage may be considerably restricted: in Norway, 6% of households receive housing allowance subsidies, whereas, a much larger percentage of households would be eligible for this support if eligibility was restricted to the relation between housing expenditure and income.

There are some typical solutions in international practice for allocating housing allowance:

- programmes restricted to the private rental sector (where rent control in the social sector results in low rents, as in Australia, for example);
- households living in areas of natural disasters are eligible;
- the scheme is restricted to households who are already the recipients of other benefit programmes (one type of allowance in Germany);
- programmes for veterans (as in Russia, for example) or students' rental programmes (in some towns in Hungary);
- only elderly or retired households are eligible for the allowance (as in some parts in Canada);
- only households of a given age group, with children, are eligible for the allowance (in Sweden between the ages of 29 and 65);
- only jobless households receive housing allowance (Ireland, United Kingdom).

Since targeting is based on means testing, states have developed all sorts of tools for testing. It is a common device to choose households that belong to the lowest 10% of the income groups, or who live on 50% or 60% less than the regional median or average income. There are also states that use a certain percentage of commonly used income categories. Whereas the first grouping reacts more sensitively to changes in the society's income conditions, the latter is based on a poverty concept which assumes that the most underprivileged group can be reduced according to a sum-based approach. A Latin American case indicates that eligibility can be based on more complex testing, namely the classification of the whole society, taking into account the population's housing situation (Colombian housing classes). Due to the great variety of means testing schemes, the coverage of housing allowance schemes shows a great variation among the countries.

In Denmark, more than 50% of the tenants get housing benefit, and 55% of the total direct budget subsidy (1997) goes to the housing benefit programme. In the autumn of 1998, the eligibility and mean-tested criteria of housing allowance schemes in Denmark were tightened in order to cut down public expenditures (Enberg, 2000). In France, nearly 50% of tenants get housing benefit (Taffin, 2003). In the United Kingdom around two-thirds of tenants receive housing benefit, and are entitled to the largest average allowance per inhabitant. In Finland, the housing allowance programme assists 21% of households, and generally demand-side subsidies[25] amount to 80% of the total housing budget (Asselin et al., 2002). A higher proportion (almost 66%) of British social tenants are dependent on housing allowances compared with the other countries (Stephens, Burns and MacKay, 2002).

### 3.6.3. "Shopping" incentive and inflationary effects on rents

The voucher system in the United States is a restricted subsidy (Priemus, 2000), and enhances certain types of housing consumption (rental and purchase), similar to rent rebates, allowances based on housing expenditure but not directly tied to housing providers (landlords or housing associations) or utility services.

"Cash" subsidies can be expended according to the specific housing expenditure (vouchers, for example). They generally enable consumers to choose from a variety of service providers (in the case of the United States, rent vouchers from landlords), steering the supply side towards competition and hence less distorting the market. Allowances that take actual expenditure into account and compensate for a given ratio of consumption can induce over-consumption and upward pressures on rents, for example. Provided that targeting is sufficient, these disadvantages can be prevented.

Shopping incentives are one of the most debated design questions of housing allowance. Some programmes (like Section 8 in the United States) incentivise tenants to negotiate or "shop" for their rent, while other

25. Housing allowances and tax deduction combined.

programmes (for example, in the Netherlands) do not make this possible (Priemus, 2000). The critics of housing allowance programmes argue that the lack of shopping incentives, for example in the British housing bene-fit scheme, encourages over-consumption. A complicated administrative mechanism has to be used to limit these upward pressures on rent expenditure (Kemp, 1997). However, housing research has not yet pro-vided clear evidence that housing allowances put upward pressure on rents (Hulse, 2002). The effects of housing allowances on the rent level depend very much on the housing market structure and the size and regional concentration of the programme.

### 3.6.4. Minimum standards

In most cases, the quality of the housing unit has to meet a minimum standard in order to close out substandard housing units. In the United States, only households choosing an appropriate standard of housing receive a voucher for rent subsidy. The aim of such standards is to motivate tenants to move out of low-standard housing to higher-quality units with higher, but subsidised rents. Some improvement in housing quality can be observed as a result of such standard-bound programmes. However, it is also obvious that similar restrictions can strongly impede participa-tion in housing programmes for the lowest income groups, ethnic minor-ities, and the elderly, for example. There are also cases – Finland, for example – where there is no minimum standard, based on the argument that this could exclude precisely those households that need support. Minimum standard requirements have been abolished in Sweden, for example, where they were considered unnecessary because of the general standard of the housing stock.

Another issue concerning setting housing standards involves the norma-tive consumption of housing, where instead of minimum levels being set, the maximum level of subsidised consumption is defined. In more mod-ern programmes, households with a higher consumption level are not excluded from the subsidy; however, their housing expenditure is only subsidised up to the defined level. Hence, the households pay for the difference between the normative expenditure and the actual expendi-ture. This feature is more progressive, as it allows for the preferences of households that favour consumption in excess of set maximum levels and allows high-quality flats to be included in the social housing programme.

### 3.6.5. Poverty trap

One of the characteristics of national subsidy systems is the phenomenon of the poverty trap. Since, in most cases, eligibility is defined according to means testing, only low-income households can access the subsidy programmes, in order to ensure better targeting. In certain areas where these limits are lower, the included households are motivated to rely on subsidies as a permanent form of income. As a result, they will not make any further attempts to access the labour market and are able to gain a higher, but less genuine, income. Besides this, income earned on the black market would also provide disincentives for households to give up the subsidy they are eligible for, according to their official income.

One negative consequence of the demand-side subsidy is that it could discourage the low-income household from increasing its labour supply. If the beneficiaries of the housing allowance programme increase their labour supply, and, as a result, their household income, the subsidy will decrease. In the United Kingdom, all recipients are completely exempt from rent rises. The steep "taper" (that determines the rate of benefit withdrawal as incomes rise) creates a poverty trap. It means that there is a disincentive to increase labour supply and household income (Murray, 1994; Schroder, 2002). Further analysis shows that the high level of housing allowance dependence and expenditure in Britain is attributable to inter-tenure polarisation, greater labour market polarisation and the lack of generosity of the social security system (Stephens, 2004).

However, there are discussions among housing researchers about how big the practical importance of the "poverty trap" of housing allowance programmes actually is. The British example is however extreme, with a taper of 100% in many cases. In most countries, the taper in the housing allowances system is lower. However, it is important to consider the total marginal effects of an increase in income by summing up marginal effects of all means tested transfers, as well as the marginal taxation of income. The total marginal effect could very well exceed 100% under some circumstances.

### 3.6.6.   Housing allowances and social segregation

Housing segregation can be both alleviated and reinforced by housing allowances. On the one hand, households receiving a housing allowance can move into housing that would have been too expensive without their allowance. In this way, there is greater freedom of choice and probably also a broader distribution of households in different residential areas. On the other hand, the allowance system can reinforce segregation: for example, if only a small portion of the housing is eligible for assistance. In this case, households receiving allowance are forced to move into these, or else are placed there by the municipality.

### 3.6.7. Financing the costs of the programme

Housing allowance programmes entail heavy budget commitments. In most cases, they are calculated in the social assistance programmes. In the economic cycle, when the economy slows down, the pressure for the housing allowances increases, as occurred in Sweden (Turner, 1997).

Hulse (2001) reports on the Canadian, United States', Australian and New Zealand housing allowance schemes' costs:

> "In Canada, the shelter assistance component of social assistance programmes was estimated at 5.2 billion Canadian dollars or 35% of total expenditure of provincial social assistance programmes in 1993 and more recent estimates put the figure as high as 50%. In the US, it was estimated that about 30% of expenditure on state social assistance programmes went on shelter payments or about US$6.5 billion in 1997. In Australia, expenditure on rent assistance was 1.54 billion Australian dollars in 1999-2000 and on the accommodation supplement in New Zealand, 0.83 billion New Zealand dollars in 1998-99."

While there is no common trend in the numbers of housing allowance claimants in the 1990s, real costs were higher at the end of the period in all countries where figures are available (Stephens, Burns and MacKay, 2002).

Sweden was the only country to have achieved significant reductions in housing allowance costs; by 1999 these had almost returned to their 1990 levels. These reductions were achieved in part by falling unemployment, but also by excluding childless claimants aged between 29 and 65 from the system. Such households could seek protection from social assistance. The major factor behind the reduction in government expenditure was the result of changes in the rules of housing allowances in order to curb the heavy expenditure increases in the 1990s (Familjeutredningen, 2001).

Although one of the basic aims of the shift from supply-side subsidies to demand-side subsidies was to overcome the fiscal constraints related to bricks and mortar subsidies, national budget balances make it obvious that this goal is still to be struggled for (see also Hulse, 2001).

### 3.6.8. Administration of the housing allowance programmes

Compared to other subsidies, managing housing allowance is complicated.

The complex set-up of the programmes influences the administrative costs of the subsidy programmes. Nonetheless, the efficiency of housing allowance schemes can best be traced with the help of co-ordinated administration and hence modifications can be more easily undertaken. The complexity of means testing, the re-examination of eligibility, and the application of minimum standards can drive up administrative costs. A further related question is the beneficiary of the scheme: housing allowances are typically paid to eligible tenants, who pay the landlord. However, there are systems where the allowance is paid directly to the landlord (as in Britain).

Besides all these considerations, the allocation of housing allowances has to be transparent in order to assure equal chances in access to the subsidy for the eligible households.

The administrative set-up of housing allowance programmes is strongly inter-related both to the characteristics of the subsidy, but also to the state administration structure. In decentralised states, where operating housing allowance is delegated to the local or regional authorities, administrative matters are also dealt with on these levels.

The table below illustrates the diversity of administrative solutions in various countries.

| Country | Administrative levels of housing allowance schemes |
| --- | --- |
| Australia | Federal government |
| Canada | Provincial governments, with some federal assistance |
| France | Central government |
| Germany | Federal scheme, administered by municipalities on behalf of the states |
| Great Britain | Local authorities, with funding from central government |
| Ireland | Regional health boards |
| Netherlands | Central government |
| New Zealand | Central government |
| Sweden | Central government |
| USA | Locally administered, in accordance with federal regulations |
| Source: Ditch et al., 2001 | |

In the case of uniform standardised systems, the state operates the allowance schemes through its decentralised organs (for example, in Germany and France). Since, in some cases, central resources contribute to the allowance schemes as well as providing for the basic legal background, the systems can be of a mixed character as well (Canada, United Kingdom, United States). Where not-for-profit organisations are also included in the operation of the housing allowance schemes, the different levels may have a wider range of responsibilities. For example, in the United Kingdom local authorities require that registered social landlords allocate at least half of their tenure to applicants from the authorities' waiting lists. At the same time, in accordance with the aims of the establishment of the social landlord structure, providers have to define the main circle of vulnerable groups as their tenants (disabled people, elderly, ethnic groups). In France, the local competence varies regionally, while social housing associations receive a lot of resources from the central budget.

### 3.6.9.    Demand-side or supply-side subsidies?

Compared to supply subsidies, demand subsidies are:

- better targeted, as they are (more or less) directly linked to the income and other characteristics of the household;

- more flexible: they can vary upward or downward with changes in income or family size, which, in particular, helps to amortise the impact of economic crises on households.

They also have a few drawbacks:

- they are a counter-cyclical burden on the budget: an economic downturn increases the number of beneficiaries and the average subsidy amount. Attempts to reduce the allowance programme can make low-income tenants insolvent – this is the dark side of their flexibility;

- they may have a "poverty trap" effect when they compensate too generously for the decrease of income due to unemployment;

- they may also have inflationary effects on rents when they are used in the private (free) sector (in the same way that incentives to investors may have an impact on housing prices). This cannot occur when rents are under strict control, which is normally the case in the social sector. It should not occur either when the households benefiting from these subsidies are a small proportion of the demand. On the contrary, when a significant number of tenants are eligible, price increases may be observed when the subsidy is introduced or improved (this was the case for students in France in 1993);[26]

- they are complex to administer, as this requires accurate and updated information on income and household composition;

- they have a limited impact on the quantity and quality of housing construction for moderate-income households; they are closely linked to the income level, not to prioritising housing need.

---

26. Laferrère & Leblanc, 2004.

On the other hand, subsidies for investors are often poorly targeted, as it is difficult to design the target accurately in terms of eligibility and priority:

- if it is too broad, it may create lifelong benefits (additional rent is seldom used) for tenants;

- if it is too narrow, there is a risk of subsidised programmes turning into ghettos.

The main advantage of object subsidies is that they are more efficient at increasing the supply of affordable housing in general and for specific target groups (such as refugees and disabled people) in particular. Also, they can be used as a counter-cyclical instrument to boost the economy or, on the contrary, be reduced when housing needs are lower or budgets tighter.

If a country considers introducing housing allowances, the best timing will probably closely depend on the general level of housing needs and their concentration on low-income households. Other factors are the ability of social landlords to self-finance their production (the proportion of the amortised stock) and liberalisation of private rents (the subsidisation is transferred from the landlords to the government).

Many countries use both housing allowances and aid to bricks-and-mortar in varying proportions, but the general trend is towards more housing allowances and fewer object subsidies, since needs are nowadays usually less important than in previous decades, and because of their technical advantages.

Can social rented housing do without object subsidies? As housing allowances have more advantages than drawbacks, why not rely solely on housing allowances whenever possible? It may be considered that, with a combination of housing allowances to tenants, tax incentives and insurance for investors for default risk of tenants, private investors should be able to provide rental housing to anyone.

However, most mature market economies still have some kind of object subsidies for the social rental sector (sometimes of a very small volume, as in the Netherlands or Spain) in addition to a more widespread housing allowance.

|  |  | Object subsidies | |
|---|---|---|---|
|  |  | Yes | No or little |
| Housing allowance | Yes | Other EU countries (15 members), Australia, Japan | Canada,* the Netherlands, Spain, the USA . |
|  | No | Belgium, Luxembourg, Portugal | Greece |

* None at the federal level; varies with the province.

Indeed, the amount of rental housing supplied by private investors is often small. Not only is it concentrated at the top end of the sector, it is also very volatile. Private investors prefer to invest in commercial property, which is more profitable and easier to manage than housing. As for individuals, they are often reluctant to house tenants whom they cannot choose themselves, or who belong to a different social group. They tend to prefer not to invest in poorly valued areas, or to accept long-term commitments. Germany provides a rare example of a social rented sector with a significant number of individuals as landlords, but the size of the sector is rapidly decreasing as is the term of their commitments.

Finally, the choice between object and subject subsidies is not only a technical choice; it also has an important political dimension. In many countries, object subsidies have been distributed for decades only by specific agents, as a special agreement is necessary to be entitled to such subsidies. These agents represent a political force, especially when they are local authorities or organisations with strong links to them. This means that changing an existing system is far more difficult than creating a new one (Taffin, 2006).

### 3.7. New directions of social housing in transition countries

The transition of 1989 to 1990 brought about a change to the political structure with introduction of the democratic political system as well as that of the market mechanism. However, these moves towards a market-based housing system took place in different ways and at different rates, and thus resulted in different sub-models. The differences can be explained partly by the exogenous factor, like the strength of the democratic institutions, structural changes and so on, and also by the endogenous factor, i.e. the institutional and legal legacy of the socialist housing system.

Even countries with relatively successful transition strategies (Hungary, Czech Republic, Poland) postponed structural changes in the public service sector such as in health, education, and the social sector, and focused on the production and financial sector. Housing was in between, because, in certain housing areas, there were no basic social barriers to major changes (construction industry, building materials), but in the area of housing services (water, heating and so on) it was not possible to introduce market mechanisms (price liberalisation, enforcement) because of the risk of creating social conflicts. The future model of the housing systems in the transitional countries depends on the policy and institutional options chosen under structural constraints (fiscal pressure, new political system, privatised economy, reformed public sector reformed and so on).

In the transition countries, the economic recession led to an impoverishment of the population in the 1990s. The decrease in GDP and real income was accompanied by increasing income inequalities. The need for social housing has increased, both in terms of helping households to pay for housing services and providing access to housing.

Under the fiscal pressure of the transitional recession, governments in the region moved out from the housing sector, terminating or cutting subsidy programmes and diminishing the direct role of the state in the housing system. Decentralisation was part of this process, as local governments were given the majority of the state-owned stock, and they managed the privatisation process.[27] As a consequence of privatisation, the share of the public stock has decreased to between 5% and 10%. There are countries like Poland, the Czech Republic and Latvia, which have a slower privatisation rate: they still have 25% to 30% of their stock public, but they failed to introduce structural changes in the public sector. (The tenants, in most of these cases, still have property rights to sell or re-let their tenancy, illustrating the lack of structural changes in the sector.)

Housing policy was faced with a huge affordability problem. In most cases, the cost of housing-related services has increased in real terms, but quite unevenly: energy costs and building materials increased the most, whilst other, mostly domestically produced services, followed the trend shortly afterwards. The prices of housing-related services increased in a period of economic decline, which resulted in accumulated arrears.

The housing stock, even at the beginning of the transition, had deteriorated, partly because of low construction and maintenance technology,

---

27. Not in Serbia or Albania, where privatisation was administered by the central government.

and partly because of under-investment in the stock before the transition. New construction declined in the transition countries to between 30% and 50% during the 1990s and it has still not reached the level of the 1980s in countries with the highest GDP in the region (Slovenia, Poland, the Czech Republic and Hungary). The housing estates in the region represent a higher percentage of the total housing stock than in western Europe – the ratio of the population in central and eastern European countries living in large housing estates reaches up to between 20% and 35% (Murie et al., 2003). This means that urban housing can be dominated by this kind of construction. In the region, housing estates represented very different technical levels, even in the period of their creation. Their deterioration accelerated after the transition, as the state moved out of the housing sector. In addition to the problem of deterioration, further elements played an important role, including the very low economic efficiency of the stock, caused by inefficient land use in urban development; huge energy problems, related to the low level of technology in construction; and low cost-efficiency in organising housing-related services (water, sewage, transportation and so on). The deterioration of the stock has speeded up in the last ten years because of the missing institutional, legal and economic conditions, which this study will discuss.

The poor performance of the housing management of multi-apartment buildings is related partly to the lack of household incentives, and partly to an inefficient use of housing wealth. The underdeveloped housing market, along with a mistrust of institutions and the uncertain legal framework, make it difficult to realise the economic and financial importance of housing wealth. But, even in the cases where households do have the incentives to realise the significance of housing wealth in the household economy, the absence of efficient intermediaries (condominiums, co-operatives, associations etc.) render such a realisation impossible (Hegedüs-Teller, 2003).

By the end of the 1990s, governments realised that the lack of social housing was causing a huge political problem. Social housing is an important element of the European housing systems. The lack of a social housing sector was considered to be a constraint to the successful accession strategy. The governments started an active programme, backed by the positive macro-economic changes. Slovakia, Romania, Hungary, Poland and the Czech Republic started programmes revitalising the social housing sector and helping the provision of affordable housing. The programme introduced new subsidies, both into the owner-occupied sector, and into public rental. Typically, these countries spent between 0.8% and

1.2% of the GDP on housing, calculating both the budget and off-budget subsidies.

Social housing programmes in the transition countries have three areas of work. The first is housing allowances or helping households to pay their housing costs (operation and maintenance). The second area is the revitalisation of the rental sector, and the third area is support for households' investment in the owner-occupied sector.[28] There has been a lot of debate about which is the most efficient method of social housing. The support to the private sector has been better accepted politically, but seems very expensive and less targeted than the social rental sector. The general view is that the countries in transition need a substantial rental sector, not only for social purposes, but also for the sake of a more mobile job market.

### 3.7.1. Housing allowances and support to low-income households

The government needs to develop a policy, which can manage the affordability issue for lower-income groups. The ways in which governments have chosen to address this issue can be divided into four strategies: 1. supply-side subsidies, which would decrease the price of services or investment; 2. modification of the tariff structure for public services, in order to help a particular type of consumer; 3. the targeting of subsidies to needy households; 4. increasing end-use efficiency, which has a long-term social impact, by reducing the cost of public services.

To solve the affordability problem, an efficient housing allowance system must be introduced in parallel with improvements in the efficiency of service provision and the enforcement system. Several countries introduced a housing allowance system in the region, affecting typically less than 10% of the population, while the share of the needy population is estimated to be between 35% and 50% (Lux, 2003; Lykova, 2003; Tshenkova, 2003). There are several reasons for this:

- lack of resources: governments under fiscal pressure try to minimise the fiscal effects of the benefit programmes;
- financial structure of the programme: most of the programmes managed by municipal governments expect local contribution. Municipal governments under fiscal pressure minimise these costs;
- the cost of the programme depends on the efficiency of the service providers; without restructuring the service provision the programmes cannot be financed.

---

28. Help in the owner-occupied sector could include subsidies for buying existing homes, constructing new units and rehabilitating existing units.

It is very important to emphasise that the housing allowance programmes should be an integrated part of the social benefit programmes. The money transferred through any benefits is fungible; thus we can suppose that a substantial part of the income benefits is spent on housing. For example, in Estonia 79.4% of the total benefit programme was spent on housing allowance in 1994, and it decreased to 20.1% in 2002 (Kahrik et al., 2003). In Hungary, the share of housing allowances was less than 4% in 2002 (Hegedüs, 2003).

### 3.7.2. Rental programmes

At the end of the 1990s, most countries in the region recovered from the transitional recession and realised that housing was an important and neglected area of politics. National housing programmes were prepared where the role of the rental sector had a high importance. Two types of rental programme were introduced.

#### 3.7.2.1. Local government programmes

The mainstream approach was the use of local governments: Slovakia, the Czech Republic and Hungary used this solution. The central government allocated grants to local governments to support rental housing programmes. The conditions were not only different in the various countries, but changed over time as well.

One issue was how the rent should be defined. The government set a ceiling to the rent for public rental units as a percentage of their "replacement value". This ceiling is 3% in Slovakia and Poland[29] and 5% in the Czech Republic. The actual rents are set by the local governments, and they are much lower than that. In Poland, for example, the average rent is around 1.5% of the replacement cost (Uchman and Adamski, 2003). In Romania, the maximum rent cannot exceed 25% of the average household income, or the household income, whichever is lower (Pascariu and Stanculescu, 2003). The regulators assumed that the local government would choose to increase the rent above this level. In Hungary, two types of the programme were introduced: social and "cost rent" programmes. The cost rent programme required a minimum rent level of 2% of the investment cost.

The programme designers were concerned with the construction cost. In Hungary, local governments had to compete for the close-ended grant, and one of the most important selection criteria in the programme was the construction cost. In Slovakia, the matching grant depended on the

---

29. The rent ceiling will be abolished in 2004, according to the plans.

construction cost. To give an incentive for lowering the construction cost, the grant was higher in the case of lower cost projects. In the Czech Republic, projects with higher costs than the ceiling are rejected. In Croatia, the government defines the maximum construction cost and land value for their programme (Čačić, 2003).

The central government defined the criteria for allocation: for example, young families, income brackets, and so on. In Slovakia, the maximum income level was set. In the Czech Republic after 2002 means testing was introduced, while in Hungary it is the responsibility of local governments to decide on the criteria.

The projected size of the programmes is substantial. In Poland, it has reached between 10% and 25% of the new construction; in Romania, it is planned to reach 40 000 units in four years (30% of the new units); in Hungary it will make up between 10% and 15% of new construction.

According to Lux (2003), in central and eastern European countries "two types of income ceilings can be distinguished: implicit and explicit. Implicit income ceilings arise from the formula used for calculating the housing allowance, whereas explicit income ceilings are strictly set in the Act. A significant change can happen when an applicant's income exceeds the ceiling because, in such a case, the applicant is not eligible for any benefit (however, this is not the case, either for the Czech or for the Polish systems). The income ceiling (with no regard as to explicit or implicit) negatively affects the household members' work incentives and leads to a poverty trap. This concerns mainly the Estonian system where one unit income growth is connected with one unit allowance decrease" (Lux, 2003).

Lux points out that in six central and eastern European countries, "with the exception of Poland, housing allowances are paid from the state budget. In Poland, *gminas* (municipalities) are mainly responsible for covering housing allowance expenses, but they obtain a grant from the state budget, calculated according to two possible, relatively complex, formulae (on average, they receive a subsidy equal to 50% of the total payment duty)" (Lux 2003) .

### 3.7.2.2. The non-profit housing association

Poland introduced a new institution for social housing, the TBS (housing associations), similar to the French 'Habitation à loyer modéré' (HLM) scheme. The TBS can take different legal forms – a limited liability company, a joint-stock company, or a co-operative of legal persons – but they cannot make a profit. The majority of TBSs are set up or initiated by local governments. The rent for TBS housing is set by the municipal councils as a cost rent; but cannot be higher than 4% of the construction cost (replacement value) of a unit, set by the *voivoda* (head of the regional council) in its quarterly edicts. The total income from rent payments for all dwellings owned by a TBS must cover all maintenance and repair costs, as well as repayment of a qualified loan from the National Housing Fund (cost rent). The explicit rules for allocating new rental flats and income ceilings were introduced by a special act (Lux, 2003).

There is a discussion in Poland about the effect of the TBS. The TBS programme was blamed for the low output of municipal housing construction, because it has left new municipal construction (MHS) virtually without resources. The government was more eager to develop a sustainable housing programme it could control, than to subsidise the construction of substandard social ghettos (Zawislak, 2003). It would facilitate the moving of better-off municipal tenants from municipal stock to TBS stock. It was also expected that the number and quality of social dwellings for the disadvantaged and the evicted would grow as a result.

The conclusion is that TBS non-profit housing associations provide good standard housing with controlled rents, but this type of housing is too expensive for the lowest income households ("affordable" sector). Meanwhile, the existing social stock is insufficient to bridge the supply gap in the "true social" sector. Expanding this sector would make it socially acceptable and politically viable to relax rental regulations.

The size of the programme depends very much on the housing fund's resources. In 2001, 10 000 TBS dwellings were built, which is between 10% and 15% of new construction.

### 3.7.2.3. Public-Private Partnership – programmes

The possibility of using the private sector for social housing is open to the transition countries. A version of PPP was introduced in Bosnia-Herzegovina. An Austrian not-for-profit organisation invested in a social rental building on the basis of a long-term (30 years) lease agreement with the government of Sarajevo Canton. The annual rent, defined as 5% of the project value, is being paid by Sarajevo Canton, as a leaseholder, from the budget revenue of the canton. (The monthly rent, paid by the tenants per square metre, will be €2.5, and the average rent €125 per apartment (Dzepar-Ganibegovic, 2003).

In Hungary, the government is reviewing a proposal to give a rent allowance to households in the private rental sector. The building companies and private investors are looking for investment possibilities with low risk.

### 3.7.3. Social programme in the owner-occupied sector

After the large-scale privatisation programmes in the region, social housing policy had to find techniques to help households to access owner occupation. The task was to design programmes targeted at low-income groups, helping them to access owner occupation, or to help low-income households improve their housing conditions through renewal and reconstruction. However, most of the countries in the region had to deal with the problems of middle and even upper-middle-income households. Because of the collapse of the housing finance system in the region, even these groups had an affordability problem. The introduction of support for saving banks, interest rate subsidies, and tax allowances, not only served first of all the higher income groups, but also created a huge fiscal burden for the governments. The Slovak and the Czech government pay between 30% and 50% of their budget subsidies to the Bausparkasse institution, supporting middle-class savings.

Very different subsidy schemes were introduced to support households in the owner-occupied sector.

The most important concern of the housing policy was to offer affordable loans for middle-income households. Mortgage programmes aim to reduce the effective interest rate paid by the borrower from a market rate.[30] Tax allowances can be used beyond supporting mortgage loans,

---

30. One typical solution was using a *special fund* to issue loans at a below-market rate of interest. Different solutions were used, including the revenues from privatisation (Estonia, Slovenia). In Slovakia, the Housing Development Fund issues a loan for the eligible client at the discount rate of the National Bank in Slovakia (Zapletalova, et al., 2003). In Poland, the National Housing Fund gives loans for TBS at an interest rate equal to 50% of the discount rate. In principle, the "solidarity fund" in Serbia belongs to this category, which is based on a wage tax. However, the typical solution is offering funding from the general budget at below-market rates.
Mortgage programmes used interest rate subsidies to reduce the effective interest paid to a private bank. Several variations were used, for example, paying the bank a fixed amount of interest. In Hungary, between 1994 and 1999 3% buy-down was used in the first five years of the loan, or some proportion of the interest or repayment (interest and amortisation) due (like 50% in a condominium rehabilitation loan in Hungary) or down to some specific rate (for example, 6% for mortgage loans in Hungary after 2001). The reduction in rate (buy down) can be for the life of the loan, or for some shorter period, or can be phased out over time.
Another technique to reduce the effective rate is the introduction of tax advantages. Personal income tax can be reduced by the amount of interest (or other payment) paid on a loan used to finance the purchase or expansion of a dwelling, occupied by the taxpayer.

for decreasing the transaction cost of the mobility, or property tax payment. In Poland, for example, eligibility is defined very broadly, so the tax can be reduced by expenditures connected with a purchase, or construction of a new dwelling (land cost included), for the renovation and modernisation of buildings, and by savings in a special housing account (Uchman and Adamski, 2003).

Among the homeownership programmes, state support for saving was very popular in the region. The contract saving schemes are designed after the German models. The households receive a bonus based on the amount saved each year, but it can only be withdrawn after a minimum number of years. This scheme was introduced in Slovakia (1993), the Czech Republic (1994), Hungary (1997) and Croatia (2000), but not in Poland.

A lump sum subsidy is a cash grant applied to housing investment by individual households. It is typically used for new investment, but can be given for reconstruction or even as a supporting transaction. The lump sum grant is used in Hungary for supporting families with children (new construction)[31] and it is given to the condominiums for rehabilitation, especially for "thermal rehabilitation". In Poland, the National Housing Fund can give up to 10% of the investment cost, a lump sum subsidy for the TBS investment.

Along with special financing schemes, specific areas, strongly related to the regional housing stock characteristics, have been developed and applied to a greater or lesser degree. One of the targets is to improve the technological characteristics of the housing stock, reduce energy consumption and stop dilapidation. The emerging and therefore quite altering interventions focus mostly on prefabricated housing. For example, in Hungary, the state provides lump sum subsidies of up to between a third and half of the total renovation costs (the co-financing has to come from both the territorial local governments and the owners), or interest rate subsidies. Poland provided personal income tax relief on the cost the

---

Mortgage insurance and guarantee. To introduce an efficient housing finance system, the role of mortgage insurance is critical. Up until now, the programme has not been very successful, because setting up a government-sponsored agency to manage the risk was thought to be difficult and was assumed not to be helpful to the financial institutions. In Estonia, after abolishing the Housing Fund, a self-managing guarantee fund, the KredEx, was established in 2000, within the administrative field of the Ministry of Economy. It guarantees housing loans for purchase by special groups and loans for condominiums (Kahrik et al., 2003).

31. In Hungary, between 1994 and 2000, a special programme was launched to help Roma people access a lump sum home ownership grant, required to organise the construction. The local governments provided the land, an NGO organised the project, and the central government supported the NGO by giving the lump sum grant to the beneficiaries.

owner (or tenant) used to repair or renovate his flat. The scheme finished at the end of 2005, after three years of operation. In addition, the investors responsible for heating renovation may apply for a 25% loan reduction – or heating efficiency improvement premium – from the Thermo-Renovation Fund. There is only limited interest in this scheme, since most modernisation work is carried out by home owners or co-operatives (Węcławowicz et al., 2004).

In Russia, families in need who are on a waiting list (for public housing) may get a lump sum subsidy for constructing or purchasing a home. The amounts and the thresholds of eligibility differ from region to region.

The question of targeting the owner-occupied sector is critical in the housing programme. In rental programmes, targeting is very important as well; however, it can be improved over time, while if the owner-occupation programme has not been targeted, the grant is lost for the social sector. Targeting techniques could include the following:

– means testing: the income and wealth test could help; however, it could be very difficult to introduce it in countries where more than 30% of the GDP is not taxed. The solution is not to give up means testing, but rather to improve income measurement;

– proxies are used to substitute or supplement the income test. The number of children and their age are used more frequently, as the financial situation of the household correlates with these variables. Young families and first-time buyers are among the typically used categories;

– the value of the subsidised unit could be a criterion for eligibility. Houses above a certain limit (in terms of their square metres per capita or value) are not eligible for the subsidies. The rationale behind this is that high-income groups are heading towards more expensive units;

– the type of building or the type of investment could limit high-income groups' access to subsidies. Prefabricated housing, for example, is mostly inhabited by lower-income groups. The rehabilitation of run-down urban areas could be another example. Most of the home ownership programmes are used for new housing, which might have a regressive income effect.

### 3.7.4. Housing areas and segregation

The focus on housing and segregation should not only deal with housing, but also with the housing environment. This has been clearly stated in Sweden, for example.

In a report to the Swedish government called *Welcome to the housing market!* the National Board of Housing, Building and Planning (2005) writes:

> "Sweden is a segregated society, which is more obvious in some parts of the country. Both the types of housing and tenure forms are to a large extent separated, which influences the distribution of groups of households, especially the socio-economic and ethnic distribution. The efforts that are being made today to break up the segregation are primarily aimed at strengthening households when it comes to education, health, employment etc. This is important work but, parallel to this, the National Authority for Building and Planning is of the opinion that it is necessary to actively work to *improve the living environment in the less attractive housing areas* and thus contribute to more equal conditions and efficiently functioning housing areas, where people want to stay and can feel proud over their housing situation."

Among the recommendations are the following:

- strengthen housing allowances so that they also include larger households in need of larger dwellings;
- Investment support for new investment and renovation, which currently focuses on smaller dwellings, should be extended to become an incentive to build larger dwellings.

## 4.    Conclusion

On the basis of the overview of the housing policies and subsidy programmes helping vulnerable social groups we can formulate some of the most important dilemmas of future programmes.

### 4.1.    Basic trends

We found two basic trends in the last two to three decades in the provision for social housing. Firstly, there has been a clear shift in the subsidy programmes from supply-side subsidies towards demand-side subsidies. Housing research has provided sufficient evidence that demand-side subsidies are more efficient than supply-side subsidies (Green and Malpezzi, 2003; Mayo, 1999; Dübel, 2000). However, economists argue that, in a restricted supply situation, subsidies on the demand-side would tend to drive up house prices (Holmans et al., 2003). The fact is that supply-side subsidies are still important elements of the low-cost housing programmes.

Secondly, there is a restructuring process in the government of social housing, in which non-government and private parties are playing an increasingly important role (Boelhouwer, 2000). However, we could conclude that national housing policies differ very much and, in several cases, they are using supply-side subsidy schemes and direct institutional solutions for good reason. The special programme targets, the state of the local housing market and the existing institutional settings determine the best solutions for social programmes. There are no cross-national recipes. Because of the historical differences in social sectors, it is not easy to summarise this trend in one paragraph. The substantial point is that either the function of social housing is taken over by new non-profit or private institutions (as in the United Kingdom), or the existing non-profit institutions are going to change, and become more independent and market-oriented organisations. The story of Dutch housing associations is a good case in point. The housing associations in the Netherlands have become more independent, but there are clear ties between the housing associations and the government. There are new proposals, which try to loosen these ties more. The question is, what would be the minimum criteria for social housing (Priemus, 2003)? Another option is to set up a new system of social housing, as the United Kingdom did, beginning in the 1970s.

## 4.2.    Definition, size and evaluation of the subsidy programmes

One of the key – but at the same time debated – elements in housing policy is subsidy. Housing policies can be evaluated according to the size of the housing subsidies, compared to the GDP. However, the measurement of subsidies is highly debated. There is no agreement on the formal definition for housing subsidies, and there is no consensus on the question of what can be reckoned as subsidy and what cannot (Haffner and Oxley, 1999). In addition to government transfer payments, cross-subsidies (off-budget transfers from one group of taxpayers to another), preferential loans provided directly or indirectly, tax allowances, and general and specific income support, can be classified as housing subsidies.

There is a vast literature on defining subsidies (Hughes, 1979; O'Sullivan, 1984,1986; Hancock and Munro, Wood, 1986, 1992; Haffner and Oxley, 1999). From the point of view of housing programmes for vulnerable households, the basic problem is the dividing line between the general income support programmes and housing-related income transfers (such as housing allowances). On the one hand, the argument is that the general income programmes have an effect on housing expenditure, because a certain proportion of this income helps the household to buy housing services. For example, in the United States, Earned Income Tax Credit provides income tax credit for millions of low- and moderate-income households[32] (Bratt, 2003). Naturally, households have to spend a certain part of this tax credit on housing. Grigsby and Bourassa (2003) argue that housing vouchers (Section 8 programme) in the United States work as an income support programme, because they do not increase the housing consumption of households, as they spend the same amount on housing they would have spent without the voucher. Thus, the amount of the voucher works as an income support programme (the money is fungible). For these reasons, it is almost impossible to compare housing allowance systems separately from income support programmes.[33]

The methodology of the calculation of the size of subsidies is debated as well. For example, in the case of an interest rate subsidy, how can we calculate the related public expenditure? One solution is to calculate the budget outlay; another solution is the present value calculation (CBO, 2004). In addition, the opportunity cost of the government can be calculated, thus the cost and expenditure dichotomy can be more clearly specified and explained. Benchmarking also raises methodological problems.

Very few studies have been published with comparative data on the size of the subsidy in the economy. Maclennan et al.. (1997) divided EU nations into four groups according to the size of the subsidies in the GDP. The first group of countries comprises those that operate with large social sectors (the United Kingdom, the Netherlands, and Sweden), spending around 3% of their GDP on housing. The second group of countries spends between 1% and 2% of their GDP on housing (Austria, Germany, France, and Denmark). The third group contains the southern European countries with large owner-occupied sectors, spending less than 1% of their GDP on housing policy (Spain, Portugal and Greece). The fourth is a residual, disparate group that has large owner-occupier markets, relatively small social sectors, and commit 1% of their GDP to housing (Ireland, Italy, Belgium, Finland and Luxembourg).

---

32. 4.8 million persons in 2002 – most of the very low-income households would be eligible for the EITC (Bratt, 2003).
33. Bradshaw and Finch (2003) developed a special method for comparison ("model family method"), where they standardised the social benefits for certain household types before the comparison.

## 4.3. Evaluation of subsidy programmes

Hoek-Smit and Diamond (2003) defined the criteria for the subsidy programmes:[34]

- efficiency: to compare the effective cost of the programme with the benefits of the programme;[35]

- equity: to measure the redistribution effect on the income groups;

- transparency: to make the cost and the benefits visible for the parties involved;

- distortions: to minimise the distortion of the behaviour of the housing market parties involved;

- administrative simplicity: to minimise the cost to the government of administering the programme.

The problem these criteria present is that they allow considerable room for interpretation of the programmes. The key question of the low-income programmes is the direct and indirect selection of the eligible clients. For example, in the case of French social housing there is an upper income limit for applicants (determining their eligibility for HLM housing), and a rental ceiling imposing an upper limit on social landlords. These limits are set nationally for the various types of households and family types, and are then adjusted according to geographical location. The current income limits allow two-thirds of the population to access social housing.

However, their social targeting is often questionable, as it is difficult to design the target properly in terms of eligibility and priority. If it is too wide, it may create life-long benefits (additional rent is seldom used) for tenants; if it is too narrow, there is a risk of turning the housing area into ghettos (Taffin, 2003).

Subsidies for investors often use subsidised loans as a privileged vehicle; in many cases, such subsidies create long-term liabilities (including credit risk) for the state. Subsidies to selected purchasers will only displace problems if there is no corresponding increase in the supply of homes. Unless the supply of homes for low-cost home ownership can be increased, the demand for social housing will grow markedly.

---

34. The study focused on housing finance subsidies. However, these are general conclusions that could be useful for our analysis.
35. We have seen before that measurement issues have not yet been solved; i.e. evaluating efficiency is a very complicated task.

## 4.4.　Institutional options: governance

A recent study of the European Central Bank, on the basis of the report by the National Central Bank, published the public expenditure on housing as a percentage of the GDP (ECB, 2003). Their data covers only the expenditure on public housing. The data in this study is not identical to that of the Maclennan et al. (1997) study. Finland, Spain, and Austria have the highest public housing expenditures (between 1.3% and 1.4% of the GDP), while Sweden, the Netherlands and the United Kingdom have much lower figures (0.6% to 0.7% of the GDP). This study admits that the data on public expenditures are not comparable, and are used to show the trend in each of the countries (ECB, 2003).

The main conclusion of the report is that housing programmes for vulnerable groups have to be embedded in national housing programmes. However, national housing policies define these groups on a wide scale: from the most vulnerable homeless people to "key workers" (middle-class families facing affordability problems). The needs of particular parts of the vulnerable social group – such as the elderly, ethnic minorities, one-parent households, people with disabilities, key workers, first-time buyers, and so on – require special programmes embedded into national housing policies.

The housing policies of low-income, vulnerable social groups are giving more and more priority to mixed neighbourhoods. The concentration and segregation of the disadvantaged groups in poor neighbourhoods has been viewed as one of the challenges of social housing policies. The intervention to the "efficient market systems" seems to be a generally accepted solution to break the vicious circle of the reproduction of poor neighbourhood. The key challenge is to develop special housing programmes to help reintegrate these segregated social groups into the society (labour market, equal access to public services, etc.).

One of the policy options in solving the housing problems of the vulnerable social group is the choice between the rental (social rental sector) and owner-occupied (low-cost housing) solution. The mixture of tenures could help create a social mix bringing about the integration of the poor households. The concentration and segregation of vulnerable or low-income households in the same area generates additional problems of social deprivation and weakened social cohesion. Mixing the tenure structure (that is, including low-cost owner-occupied units) can help achieve stable neighbourhoods rather than "welfare ghettos" which stigmatise their occupants. Housing programmes for vulnerable social groups – if they exist – are embedded in the national housing and social programmes. Special attention should be given to the relationship between special housing programmes and social (income, unemployment benefit) programmes. Social programmes are increasingly complex, and housing is only one element of the policy to help integrate disadvantaged groups.

In the transition countries, the governance of social housing has been a critical element in social housing programmes. The collapse of the centrally planned economy led to the collapse of the institutions providing social housing. New institutions have to be set up, or the behaviour and the operation of the old institutions has to be changed. There are huge pressures on governments to provide sustainable social housing.

There are different solutions across the region, but the typical one is to set up a government agency[36] – something like a national housing fund – such as was established in Slovakia (1996), Romania (1999), Poland (1993) and Estonia (1995), for example. However, social programmes are run through the "window" institutions in other countries (in Hungary, for example, public institutions are set up under the department responsible for managing housing programmes). The agencies or public institutions are under the executive control of the ministries, but they may have other roles as well. The preparation of housing programmes, the financial management of the programmes, monitoring results and controlling the operation may also be their responsibility. The agencies in the region have the potential to develop from being "de-concentrated" government units towards being semi-private institutions, competing or co-operating with the private sector, responsible for issuing and/or guaranteeing mortgage bonds as a primary source of funding and lending it to the customers backed by the collateral.

Thus, local governments typically play an important role in running social housing programmes. The successes of the programmes are the incentives built into the grant structure. As a consequence of decentralisation, a significant part of the housing responsibility was transferred to local governments, and they have relatively broad expenditure autonomy. The local governments in the region developed different models towards an efficient social housing policy, some of them related to the central programmes, some of them independent from them. We should emphasise

---

36. Housing is quite a complex area of public policy, so it is not easy to put all the tasks under one ministry or agency. Thus the co-operation among the ministries related to housing issues (from building laws to banking regulations) is crucial, which again can be the task of this agency or department. In Hungary, the housing issues floated among various ministries, and have now settled at the Ministry of the Interior as an independent section. However, the housing allowance is under the Ministry of Social Welfare.

here that some of the countries in the region had a very fragmented system of local government (the Czech Republic, Slovakia and Hungary, for example). Not-for-profit organisations could give a new impetus to social housing efforts. Social care institutions in particular, have stakes in the future of the social sector. They are very under-developed as yet, but represent an alternative.

This report has focused on describing the different subsidy programmes, although the general national housing policy environment is very important. This is especially true in the transition countries where the institutional background of efficient housing systems is just being formed (privatisation of the banking system, the legal background of an effective housing finance system and so on). The relation between special programmes and the national housing policy is crucial. A specialised programme cannot be efficient and politically feasible if the fundamentals of the housing system are not addressed. In the case of the developing countries, the "enabling housing" policy suggestion of the World Bank is important (World Bank, 1993). The housing policy in the transition countries first has to address the demand- and supply-side constraints of the housing market (property rights, mortgage finance, subsidy structure, land policy and building regulations). A typical problem of social housing is the relation of special social programmes to national housing programmes.

In order to execute Article 31 of the European Social Charter, particularly with regard to homelessness prevention, the final report should include a definition of the following target housing policies:

— as a general objective, preventing persons that have adequate housing from the loss of their housing, through the following means:

- secure legal certainty of tenants and transparency when renting the flats;

- secure firm and permanent tenancy, with a special emphasis on the prevention of unnecessary and premature tenancy termination;

- reduce the scope and number of reasons for eviction, either in public or private flats, taking into account justifiable interests of the landlords;

- influence the price of rented property, so that it is affordable to those with insufficient means (which is an explicit obligation of states according to Item 3, Article 31, Part II of the ESC);

- prevent price increase in rented property.

To abolish the reasons that stem from the country sphere, the activities of the countries should primarily be focused on the following:

- active regulation, by statute, of the tenancy sector, as regards the design, permanence and stability of tenancies, so that stability and permanence are secured for tenancies, and, above all, to reduce the reasons for premature evictions and the unnecessary termination of tenancy;

- rent regulation, by introducing a reasonable upper limit so that the amount is not determined only at the discretion of the landlord, while its concept would be correlated with the landlord's cost of instruction, maintenance cost and provide a certain profit if it is necessary;

- abandonment of any exacerbation of the tenants' position, via amending the legislation and deregulating or abandoning the existing rent regulation.

With all that said, we should also consider the justifiable and protected interests of landlords, whereby Property right versus Housing right would prove to be a topical issue. Here we could consider the exhaustive court practice of the European Court of Human Rights in Strasbourg that deals in detail with the extent to which the state is allowed to restrict ownership rights on account of tenants' protection.

To abolish the reasons that stem from the sphere of individuals, the states should introduce an efficient system of subsidising individuals who do not have enough means of their own.

## 5. Dimensions of evaluation

The evaluation of housing policies and applied measures is one of the key elements in assessing the effects of applied national techniques on targeted vulnerable groups. Nevertheless, national housing policies contain numerous elements that have more targets and aim at completing various goals.

In the following section, we focus on a set of dimensions that enable the policy makers to evaluate housing policy measures according to their effects on vulnerable groups.

### 5.1. Measurement of targeting

As discussed in section 3.5, there have been extensive discussions on policy interventions and their effects on given layers of society and the housing market. Among these – at times controversial – debates, targeting is one of the key topics. Different economical approaches emphasise subsidising the supply side, in order to push prices down, others rather concentrate on preventing the leakage of subsidies and hence force specified targeting means. Another aspect of targeting measurement is also strongly related to the filter-down effect. This phenomenon describes the dynamics of the upward or downward mobility of the given stock, and thus of the population that gains access to the vacant housing from which the better off typically have moved further to higher value areas.

Independent of the tools, however, the support that has been invested in different housing related programmes by governments or local governments, for example, should always be evaluated according to the need of the vulnerable for such supports.

Besides mapping and reflecting the needs of the vulnerable for specific housing support, the quality of the thus affordable or accessible housing stock should be measured, in order not to reproduce vulnerable areas or deteriorating stock and push the vulnerable into this housing. Hence, setting a minimum standard of housing should provide for a benchmark to measure targeting.

## 5.2.    Institutional design

International examples prove that policy interventions imply the development of institutional structures that are responsible for managing, implementing and monitoring the measures. In countries of transition, in particular, the institutional design is one of the key elements of a sustainable programme implementation, and its importance should not be underestimated elsewhere. The countries show a great variety of institutional set-ups, and it is clear that there are numerous factors that serve as dimensions of the institutional set-up and should be taken into account when evaluating the institutional design of interventions:

- risk and benefit sharing among the interested partners, including whether the given stakeholders have a set of controlling tools for each other;
- types of incentives that are associated with the measure, in order for the parties to get and stay involved in the programme (especially to enhance PPP);
- costs of administration are controlled and low;
- the institutional set-up provides for sufficient monitoring and is capable of a decent evaluation of the programme;
- the institutional parties have a solid and consistent legal basis (including planning regulations) for acting.

## 5.3. Long-term effects

Policy measures are designed to meet both short and long-term effects. Each evaluation should therefore deliver a set of intended long-term effects that serve as a basis for judging the measure's effectiveness. Measures for vulnerable groups, in particular, and changes in their housing situation should focus on numerous elements, besides the achievement of long-term goals and compliance of the measure with other elements of the housing policy (avoiding of contradictory interventions and negative side-effects) such as:

– minimisation of the negative effects of housing subsidies (for example, capitalisation);
– development of cohesion due to the measure (access to jobs, education etc.);
– sustainability of the measure in terms of central/local government finances;
– safety of deterioration of the constructed/accessed housing stock;
– enhancement of choices available to households;
– the long-term effects should be also viewed in the framework of an ideal model of a market with as few as possible distortions.

## 5.4. Nature of measure

Our report stresses that there is a wide variety of types of measures, and one of the most important outcomes of our international comparison is that similar goals can be achieved through diverse actions. Some measures may be, however, more appropriate under certain economic and housing market circumstances. Therefore, the nature of the measures should be investigated from at least three perspectives:

– What benefits have grants as opposed to subsidies over time (and vice versa) in the case of the given goal and the target group?
– How complex is the measure in terms of combining the housing elements with further structural aspects such as jobs, education, health and community development? Is the measure sustainable without the associated interventions?
– Is the measure adequate and flexible to address future emerging problems (e.g. changing housing aspirations)?

## 5.5. Tenure structure

There have been extensive discussions on international forums, among academics and policy makers, on differences that emerge based on different set-ups of welfare regimes. The European case shows that social housing – as one of the key tools for low-income households to have access to secure housing – has on the one hand become residual over the last decades; on the other hand, the scarcity of vacant housing or housing that matches demand of low-income families pushes more households towards the private rental or owner-occupied sector. Governments therefore have broadened their subsidy schemes both towards private rentals and home ownership, which has resulted in manifold assistance programmes and interventions. In order to enhance social cohesion, measures that foster access to a diversity of types of housing tenures should be prevalent, unless the short-term goal of the measure is to favour a given type of tenure (for example, social housing).

Different tenure types tend to have different costs of access. Once a measure is designed to improve mobility through lowering transaction costs, the preventative actions and interventions needed to avoid negative side-effects (such as neighbourhood deprivation and segregation as richer households move away) also need to be taken into account.

## 5.6. Integration

Measures for vulnerable groups aim at enhancing integration. Therefore any such measure should be evaluated taking into account integration on a physical, cultural, educational and employment level as well, as design- related interventions.

While exploring different types of expected integrative effects, the focus should be on lowering vertical inequality and decreasing distance among tenures.

## 5.7. Piloting

Elaboration of measures has numerous phases, among which piloting is essential, in order to test unwanted results and avoid exacerbated financial burdens. Therefore, measures should be piloted or initially implemented as trial projects, on the basis of which the thresholds of eligibility or other parameters can be modified.

On the whole, measures have similar counterparts in other countries, which means that relevant international experience should be drawn on while designing the given intervention and evaluating its pilot phase.

Piloting, as a phase of implementation, might have an influence on the target group's behaviour in terms of trust and distrust in the stability of a given programme. Opening up and fostering restrictions therefore have to be carefully designed, and both the parties who get involved in the pilot phase, and those who are excluded, should be made aware of the fact that further modifications of the programme are likely, following the experimental phase.

### 5.8.  Vulnerable groups (see table, p. 74)

Due to the diversity of housing policy structures and measures (which should be considered in the context of the national housing market and local housing problems) the beneficiary groups which can be identified differ from place to place. Nevertheless, according to in-depth mapping of the existing housing sector and of those who have housing problems, the policy makers have to choose from various alternative interventions:

- Is the vulnerable group affected indirectly by targeting housing problems (for example, affordability)?
- Is the vulnerable group affected directly (identified as the target group)?

### 5.9.  Understandability of the programme

International experience shows that the targeting of measures can be very well designed; nevertheless, certain eligible groups will not participate and benefit from the programmes. This phenomenon might have numerous reasons, among which we should stress the lack of clarity of the given programme. The target group must see the prerequisites for its participation and the benefits it could gain from this participation. In the case of decentralised programmes in particular, the institutional set-up has to be designed in a way that allows for smooth communication with the target group and the target group must have trust in the institution that communicates the conditions of the programme.

### 5.10.  Behaviour of the target group

The effectiveness of a measure very much depends on its behavioural influence on the target group. If the measure aims at raising housing consumption, by providing additional resources (such as housing allowance or mortgage subsidy), for example, it is of utmost importance – from the perspective of effectiveness – that the beneficiaries use the subsidy for housing, not for other consumption or wealth accumulation purposes. In this way, the quality of housing consumption is raised. Therefore, changes in behaviour of the target group have to be evaluated in the light of the goals of the measure.

The following matrix demonstrates the dividing line between the two approaches:

## Matching vulnerable groups with housing problems (Hungary)

| Vulnerable groups (sample list) | Housing problems | | | | | | Interventions |
|---|---|---|---|---|---|---|---|
| | Low housing quality and consumption | Access to home ownership is difficult | Affordability problems | Small social housing sector | Deteriorating neighbourhoods | Low mobility | |
| Elderly | | | X | X | X | X | Housing allowance, social housing |
| One-parent households | | X | X | X | X | X | Housing allowance and special guarantees |
| Low-income households | X | X | X | X | X | X | Social housing, housing allowance and special guarantees |
| Key-workers | | X | | X | | X | Social housing, housing allowance and special guarantees |
| Ethnic minorities | X | X | X | X | X | X | Settlement rehabilitation programmes |
| People with disabilities | X | X | X | X | X | X | Housing allowance, and refurbishment programmes |
| Homeless people | | X | X | X | | X | Social housing, etc. |
| | Interventions | | | | | | |
| | Subsidies for renovation and infrastructure development | Mortgage subsidies, lump sum subsidies, etc. | Housing allowance schemes | Social housing construction, establishing non-profit actors in housing | Complex rehabilitation and neighbourhood renewal programmes | Lowering transaction costs | |

74

## 5.11.  Continuity

A further key element of the measure is its continuity, which can be based on the lessons learned during its piloting phase. Continuity, too, allows for the measure's smooth integration into the housing subsidy system of the given country or community. It is this feature which establishes trust on the part of the target group; thus it is essential to achieve this for a sustainable programme.

## 5.12.  Acceptance of the programme

As well as being embedded in the housing subsidy system of a given country or community, the measures should be accepted both on the part of the target group and generally by the society, since it is mostly the middle class that finances such programmes through its taxes.

Nevertheless, the target group's acceptance of the programme should be largely emphasised in terms of belief and trust that the given measure will have a positive impact on their housing situation, thereby enhancing cohesion and integration.

# 6.  Recommendations

Based on the international review of housing policies focusing on vulnerable groups, we can conclude that there are tensions and sorting processes in each society's housing system, and without appropriate preventive steps these tensions can lead to segregation and to problems that require weighty and costly interventions. International experience shows that there are applicable models working already (Norway and Finland), hence there are already systems that can be adopted in more countries.

There is an observable aim of the countries in question to solve the housing problems of both the middle classes and the vulnerable groups. This intention can be justified by the need for society-wide acceptance of quite costly housing programmes. It is also clear that housing itself is insufficient to achieve larger cohesion. On the other hand, without appropriate housing options, there is no social cohesion.

Our recommendations therefore focus on necessary steps and elements of housing policies for vulnerable groups, and take into account that housing policies should decrease the cost to society and according the Lisbon Agenda, by achieving larger cohesion, should contribute to the competitiveness of the European area.

1.       The core part of a methodology for designing housing policies should be mapping and identifying the housing problems and defining

vulnerable groups. Based on these definitions, the housing problems of vulnerable groups can be explored.

2.	Secondly, it is necessary to identify the probability that vulnerable groups have access to housing subsidies. This is a question of redistribution and allocation of the subsidies, which has to be critically evaluated.

3.	Thirdly, based on the findings, elaborated programmes have to be started, initially on a small scale, guided by monitoring, which can draw on previous and ongoing research findings. Capacity building for research has to be supported. The dimensions of evaluation should guide each programme design (see Section 5 of the Report).

4.	The experiences of the programme phases have to be exchanged among the stakeholders. The focus should be on actions in general.

5.	International exchange of expertise is necessary, since there are numerous existing networks which are appropriate forums for academic exchange. Professional co-operation on an international level can be established with international, political, financial and the stakeholders' support.

6.	The thus elaborated solutions should be integrated with other necessary policies in order to achieve a sustainable, complex system of measures that provide for greater cohesion.

# 7.    Appendices

## 7.1.    FEANTSA definition: Homelessness and Housing Exclusion

*Conceptual definition of homelessness and housing exclusion*

| Conceptual category | Physical domain | Social domain | Legal domain |
|---|---|---|---|
| Rooflessness | No dwelling (roof) | No private space for social relations | No legal title to a space for exclusive possession |
| Houseless | Has a place to live | No private space for social relations | No legal title to a space for exclusive possession |
| Insecure housing (adequate housing) | Has a place to live | Has space for social relations | No security of tenure |
| Inadequate housing (secure tenure) | Inadequate dwelling (dwelling unfit for habitation) | Has space for social relations | Has legal title and/or security of tenure |
| Unaffordable housing | To be defined | To be defined | To be defined |

| Conceptual category | | Operational category |
|---|---|---|
| Roofless | 1 | Living in a public space (no abode) |
| | 2 | Stay in a night shelter (forced to spend several hours a day in public space) |
| Houseless | 3 | Stay in service centre or refuge, for example:<br>– hostels for the homeless<br>– women's shelters<br>– etc. |
| | 4 | Live in temporary accommodation, for example:<br>– temporary accommodation (paid by municipality)<br>– Interim accommodation (awaiting assessment)<br>– transitional living unit (short-term lease)<br>– low-budget hotels paid by public funds |
| | 5 | Live in temporary accommodation reserved for immigrants (asylum seekers, repatriates etc.) |
| | 6 | Living in institutions:<br>– prison, care centre, hospital – have to leave within a defined period and for whom no accommodation is available |
| | 7 | Living in designated supported accommodation (without a legal tenancy contract) |

| Conceptual category | | Operational category |
|---|---|---|
| Insecure housing | 8 | Living in designated supported accommodation (where tenancy is dependent upon support to be accepted and available) |
| | 9 | Have legal enforceable notice to quit, related to landlord action or action of mortgage provider |
| | 10 | Excluded under legislation (by police order) and no place to stay<br>– Anti-social behaviour<br>– Domestic abuse legislation<br>– etc. |
| | 11 | Living temporarily with family or friends (not through choice) |
| | 12 | Living under threat of violence (from partner or family) |
| | 13 | Living in dwelling without a standard legal (sub) tenancy |
| Inadequate housing | 14 | Living in temporary structure<br>Shanty dwelling<br>Squatting |
| | 15 | Living in mobile home/caravan (which is not a legal [and thereby serviced] site or holiday accommodation) |
| | 16 | Living in dwelling which is declared unfit for habitation under (national) legislation – to be redefined |
| | 17 | Living in a dwelling which is overcrowded (according to national statutory definition) – to be redefined |
| Unaffordable housing | | To be defined |

## 7.2. Composition of the Group of Specialists CS-HO

*Bulgaria*

Mrs Rumyana Petrova
Chief expert in "Strategic Planning of Regional Policy" Directorate
Ministry of Regional Development and Public Works
17-19 St. Kiril I Metodii Str.
1202 Sofia

*Czech Republic*

Ms Hana Zelenková
Ministry of Labour and Social Affairs
na Poříćním právu 1
128 01 Prague 2

*France*

Mme Anne-Marie Fribourg
Chargée de Mission
Ministère de l'équipement, des transports, de l'aménagement du
territoire, du tourisme et de la mer
Direction générale de l'urbanisme, de l'habitat et de la construction
Service du Développement urbain et de l'habitat
Arche de la Défense Paroi Sud
92055 La Défense Cedex

*Germany*

Mr Adolf Völker
Referatsleiter, Referat SW 31
Förderpolitik im Wohnungswesen, Mietenpolitik, Eigentumspolitik
Bundesministerium für Verkehr, Bau- und Stadtentwicklung (BMVBS)
Invalidenstrasse 44
10115 Berlin

*Italy*

Mr Pietro Tagliatesta
Representative of Italy to the European Committee for Social Cohesion
Funzionario, Ministero del Lavoro e delle Politiche sociali
Via Flavia 6
0187 Rome

*Norway*

Mrs Anne-Margareth Kaltenborn Lunde
Senior Adviser
Ministry of Local Government and Regional Development
Housing and Building Department
P.O. Box 8112 Dep.
0032 Oslo


*Romania*

Mr Teofil Oliver Gherca
Expert
General Division for Urban and Territorial Planning
Ministry of Transport, Construction and Tourism
38, Dinicu Golescu, Bvd. Sector 1
Bucharest 010873


*Russian Federation*

Mr Alexander Razumov
All-Russian Centre for Living Standard Studies
4-aya parkovaya ul. 29
105043 Moscow


*Non-governmental organisations*

Mr Freek Spinnewijn
Fédération Européenne des Associations travaillant avec les Sans-Abris
(FEANTSA)
Klein Drogenhofstraat 1
3210 Lubbeek
Belgium

Ms Mateja Tamara Fajs
International Union of Tenants (IUT)
Government of the Republic of Slovenia
Office for Legislation
Mestni trg 4
1000 Ljubljana
Slovenia

*Observer*

Ms Darinka Czischke
European Social Housing Observatory (CECODHAS)
Research Co-ordinator
59 b, rue Guillaume Tell
1060 Brussels
Belgium

*Consultant of the Group*

Mr József Hegedüs
Institute for Metropolitan Research
Varoskutatas Ktf.
Lonyay utca. 34 III.21 - Pf. 1176
Budapest
Hungary

*Contributors to the report*

Mrs Nóra Teller
Researcher
Institute for Metropolitan Research
Varoskutatas Ktf.
Lonyay utca. 34 III.21 - Pf. 1176
Budapest
Hungary

Mr Per Åhrén
Senior Adviser
Norwegian State Housing Bank
P.b. 5130 Majorstua
0302 Oslo
Norway

### 7.3. Guidelines on access to housing for vulnerable groups elaborated by the Group of Specialists on Housing Policies for Social Cohesion (CS-HO)

*I.  Introduction*

1.      Access to housing for vulnerable groups is a challenge facing all Council of Europe member states. Consequently, in November 2004, the Council of Europe set up a Group of Specialists on Housing Policies for Social Cohesion (CS-HO) whose aim was to recommend appropriate measures in some critical areas of housing policies, in order to enable vulnerable groups to access and live in adequate housing.

2.      The purpose of the CS-HO work was to formulate concrete measures and policies within the areas of supply of housing, financing and housing allowances, in order to enable vulnerable groups to have access to housing and enjoy security of tenure.

*II.  Definition*

3.      Vulnerability in the housing sector means that there are groups, persons and households who are in an inadequate housing situation, or are at high risk of becoming so.

*III.  Prerequisites for an effective housing policy for vulnerable groups*

4.      General housing policies should be clearly defined and should include special policies for vulnerable groups. These policies should be integrated with the national economic and social policies.

5.      It is necessary to reappraise and upgrade the role of the housing sector within the national development policy, with special attention given to the reviewing of existing measures helping the vulnerable groups.

6.      Effective governance of housing policies is crucial for the implementation of any measures for vulnerable groups. The role of national, regional and local authorities in housing policies should be clearly and legally defined. The institutional and administrative system of local governance should be transparent, efficient, effective, defining the role of civil society/NGOs. The system should allow participation of stakeholders. The programmes should be designed so they foster partnerships at local, regional and national levels, as appropriate, in their policies aimed at addressing the housing problems for vulnerable groups.

7.     An appropriate legal, financial and institutional base is an essential precondition for addressing the problems of vulnerable groups. The state should be actively involved in legal regulation of any housing relationships by its compulsory provisions.

8.     The relevant authorities should undertake a regular review of their housing legislation, policies and practices and remove all provisions or administrative practices that result in direct or indirect exclusion of vulnerable groups.

9.     The legal environment (rent regulation, tenancy rights, and so on) should provide balanced security, both for the tenants and the landlords. In order to prevent evictions, the states should provide adequate security of tenure for tenants, either in public or private accommodation. Tenants should be provided with adequate protection against premature termination of tenancy and arbitrary increases in rent. In the transition countries, special measures are necessary to protect the security of tenure for tenants who live in dwellings previously publicly owned and governed (sitting tenants).

10.     Legal regulation of land and housing development should be in place, in order to ensure sufficient provision of residential land and infrastructure investment. A legal system is needed which includes and specifies property, land and secure tenure rights, procedures for legal eviction and legal protection from unlawful evictions.

11.     Housing policies should be evidence-based, and therefore the knowledge base should be improved through research and regular data collection. Adequate knowledge of the housing situation, especially statistical information, is a prerequisite for effective housing policy design and implementation. Regular collection of relevant statistical information on housing issues, including housing needs assessment, should be carried out.

IV.     *Guidelines on housing policy for vulnerable groups*

12.     There is a range of potential tools for improving housing for vulnerable groups, which for the purpose of these guidelines will be considered as:

- tools aimed at increasing the supply of decent and affordable rental housing;
- tools facilitating access to housing finance for vulnerable groups;
- making effective use of housing allowances.

For different vulnerable groups, in a given national context, a specific combination of these measures may be appropriate.

*Guidelines on increasing the supply of decent and affordable rental housing*

13.     In designing programmes for the vulnerable groups, governments have to consider different measures used for providing or increasing the supply of rental housing. The programmes have to pass the viability test for measuring the real need for new housing units on the local housing market, where the needs for appropriate housing cannot be met by the existing stock in the prevailing circumstances.

14.     Abundant supply of rental housing is an effective way of improving access to housing for vulnerable groups, who often cannot afford the cost and risks of ownership.

15.     Countries with a low-level rental sector (below 20%) should consider ways to increase the supply of housing in the rental sector, especially in urban areas. In such cases, social housing should play an important role. Adequate legal, financial and tax conditions should be created, in order to encourage the supply of social rental housing.

16.     In order to increase the supply of adequate and affordable rental accommodation, the private and non-profit sector should be supported by necessary legal and financial measures. Governments should provide an adequate organisational framework and provisions in the national legislation, policies and strategies, designed to increase the supply of rental housing. Provisions should also be made for different means, forms and methods of access to housing – such as social housing, co-operatives, public housing, and innovative forms and tenures of housing. All the relevant elements of the housing models mentioned (financial, social and other) should be clearly defined.

17.     The area- and community-based programmes should be given more emphasis. Area-based grant programmes (for example, cash subsidy, tax exemption, etc.) can efficiently contribute to the rehabilitation of a distressed area and the creation of a mixed neighbourhood.

18.     In cases where supply of new housing units is necessary, a number of different public policies may be used. Typically, specific programmes use a combination of different financial measures and define their institutional framework.

19.     The housing strategy using a single or any combination of measures should be accompanied by some targeting mechanism. Targeting

aims at vulnerable groups or at distressed areas, defined by special indicators.

20.     In cases where financial incentives (tax incentive, capital grants, etc.) are used, responsibilities should be carefully allocated among the stakeholders (capital owners, developers, housing company managers and public sector authorities).

21.     The provision of a capital grant is an effective instrument for increasing the supply of housing for vulnerable groups, on the condition it is restricted to bodies that carry out a clearly defined public service obligation. The capital grant provides powerful incentives and its costs are predictable. It should be used in combination with other measures, such as housing allowances, and under a specific institutional framework, which guarantees the achievement of the programme objectives. A capital grant is the most effective instrument in cases where there are severe housing supply and social problems, in order to ensure access to housing for vulnerable groups.

22.     Tax advantages for housing providers are very commonly used financial incentives for increasing the supply of housing. The form of tax advantages varies widely, including partial or total exemption from profit tax, an accelerated depreciation of rental properties and partial reduction of VAT. The programmes should provide stable, predictable and long-term advantages for the landlord providing social housing. It may be a measure to increase supply of housing in general, but it is not necessarily targeted at vulnerable groups. Of all tax advantages, VAT reduction may be the best suited for targeting vulnerable groups.

23.     Interest rate subsidy programmes used to have a crucial importance in a high-inflation environment. They could cause undesirable market distortion, if used as a general supply instrument. Therefore, they should be well targeted at vulnerable groups. They may have an important role in the transition countries, in cases where inflation is relatively high.

24.     Mortgage guarantees for institutions which supply social housing have proved to be an efficient tool for supporting the supply of affordable housing, in a well-designed institutional environment.

*Housing finance instruments for vulnerable groups, aimed at facilitating home ownership*

25.     In countries and regions where the rental and mortgage markets are not well established, or in rural areas, policies providing access to

housing finance for home ownership might be a possible solution for facilitating access to housing for vulnerable groups.

26. The government should choose among the demand-side tools which fit into the country's legal and financial framework and which are tailored to the specific needs of vulnerable groups. Targeting is also necessary to control fiscal effects.

27. Beyond the provision of an efficient legal and institutional framework, there are a number of specific tools, which can be used to promote access to housing of vulnerable groups in the owner-occupied sector.

28. Guarantees provided by government agencies, or by private guarantee institutions, have proved to be an efficient instrument for helping low-cost home ownership programmes in a developed legal and financial environment. With such guarantee schemes, vulnerable groups have better access to credit, since the guarantees reduce the risks of loans given to low-income groups, and thus ease credit rationing.

29. Housing allowance for home buyers helps low-income households to pay their expenditures related to the new unit. This is a means tested support for vulnerable groups in the owner-occupied sector. Housing allowances are discussed in detail in the next section.

30. The capital grant is considered to be a very efficient instrument to enhance the access to housing of low-income groups in an immature housing finance environment. The advantages of this instrument are its transparency and predictability of its total cost. For well-defined target groups (e.g. first-time buyers) it could be a very efficient contribution, even in a developed housing finance system.

31. Interest rate subsidies have been very popular methods of increasing the purchasing capacity of the beneficiaries, but these instruments became less important in the low-inflation environment. Typically, these are not means tested programmes, which means that they are not targeted, unless specific eligibility criteria are used (for example, families with members who have disabilities, first-time buyers, immigrants, etc.). If targeted on vulnerable groups, these subsidies may be a useful tool for facilitating their access to housing.

32. Contract saving systems are voluntary saving products, which offer some financial incentives for savers in the form of premium, preferential loans, or tax advantages. This tool is less appropriate in a high-inflation environment and for low-income households. Such a policy tool is not recommended for helping vulnerable groups to gain access to housing, taking into account the limited potential for people on

low incomes to benefit from it and the risk of high expense for the public budget.

33.    For social groups with low access to the conventional credit tools, it might be advisable to consider the use of micro-finance schemes, which make it possible to access loans of small amounts, to be used for refurbishing of housing, or self-help housing schemes.

34.    Shared ownership, where a partial owner can gradually become a full owner, could decrease the financial burden of the targeted group, combining the advantages of owner-occupation and the rental scheme. This scheme can be combined with other tools, such as interest-free loans. However, shared ownership schemes require a special legal background and a well-developed practice.

*Guidelines on effective use of housing allowances*

35.    The goals for a housing allowance system should be to improve access to decent, affordable housing for all households on low incomes and to function as a safety net for these households against increases in housing expenditure, or decreases in income.

36.    Housing allowances are a means tested demand-side support to low-income households, which enable them to consume more housing than without the subsidy. Most countries in Europe have some type of housing allowance. This tool has, to a large extent, supplemented or replaced supply-side subsidies. Housing allowances are often considered to be more cost efficient than supply-side subsidies, because they can be easily and more effectively targeted and are more flexible, automatically adjusting to changes in household income, housing expenditure, and so on.

37.    When there is a shortage in the supply of adequate housing for low-income households, a combination of housing allowances and supply-side subsidies should be considered. The housing allowances themselves will have a minor effect, or no effect at all, on the housing supply.

38.    In order for an efficient housing allowance system to work, the following prerequisites, concerning the data, have to be in place or developed:

–    reliable data on household income level should be available as a basis for the means test;

- data on household expenditure on housing should be available. Such data is used for determining the necessary expenditure for reasonable housing consumption, for households in different situations;
- reliable data on household composition should be available, as a basis for assessing the need for allowances for households, according to household income, size and other indicators of need;
- data should be updated continuously;
- if these data are not available, proxies or indicators can be used in the design of housing allowances.

39.     A system for housing allowances should include the following elements:

- acceptable income levels, after payment of housing expenditure, should be defined for different types of households, tenures, locations and so on. These income levels will indicate the need for housing allowances for different reasonable housing expenditures. In this way, the allowances will decrease the need for support through social welfare payments;
- the amounts of allowance should be based on the needs of vulnerable households;
- a system where benefits are an increasing function of housing expenditure and a decreasing one in income. The system should minimise poverty traps and other negative effects;
- definition of maximum eligible housing expenditures for different types of households, for the calculation of the allowances.

40.     All tenures and types of households should be eligible, in order to avoid segregation and distortions in the housing market.

41.     There should be neutrality in tenures, unless the government has a reason to favour a specific tenure, for example, to enhance social cohesion by having larger housing allowances in tenures with relatively few low-income households.

42.     The housing allowance system should be co-ordinated with social policy and transfer systems.

43.     The system should be transparent, both to consumers and administrative bodies. The design of the system should avoid unnecessary complexity.

44.     Allowances should be large enough to affect behaviour of the targeted households and should be controlled effectively. Risk of "leakages" should be minimised.

45.    The allowances system should not cover 100% of the housing expenditure.

## V.    Need for integrated policies and measures

46.    Housing policies for vulnerable groups should be designed and implemented taking into account general housing policies, and policies in related sectors – such as education, health, employment, transport, urban planning and social protection. For example, social rental housing should be well connected to areas with employment and training opportunities, in order to facilitate the integration of households on low incomes with the labour market. It is important to co-ordinate efforts of the relevant authorities, to find and exploit synergies between different sectors, and to encourage the public authorities at all levels to adopt comprehensive approaches and policies.

47.    A legal framework, supporting the system of housing policy, should be set up or revised in order to give transparent, contractual agreements between the different parties, legal provisions regarding security of tenure and security of ownership, a legal framework for financial laws, land and mortgage laws, bank regulations, administrative and procedural laws – including laws on forced evictions, rental laws, laws on various forms of planning, partnerships, and housing types (as condominiums and co-operatives).

48.    Integrated housing measures have to be developed for specific vulnerable groups. The definition and social composition of vulnerable groups differs from country to country, thus it is important that the governments develop specific programmes addressing the housing problems of these groups.

49.    The housing measures of these programmes should use a combination of the methods developed under the previous headings and should include the building or development of the entire physical and social infrastructure, that is needed for adequate and sustainable housing.

50.    Besides the central level, regional and local authorities should also develop housing policies, strategies and action plans, coping with special local housing problems and taking into consideration the possible roles of the private sector and non-governmental agencies.

51.    An efficient and transparent institutional structure, including administrative procedures on all levels and defining the role of all parties involved in the housing policies, should be developed.

52.     NGOs, especially those working with or representing the interests of vulnerable groups, should be involved in the process of conceiving, designing, implementing and monitoring policies and programmes, aimed at improving their housing situation.

*VI.     Housing policy measures and their contribution to social cohesion*

53.     The objective of housing policy should be to ensure access to affordable housing with an adequate standard, to ensure the security of housing for all, and to enhance social cohesion. The design of new, and the evaluation of existing housing policies should also be done from the perspective of social cohesion. The importance of social cohesion should be acknowledged among all stakeholders.

54.     There has not been much focus on social cohesion in the discussion and implementation of housing policies in the past. There are some housing policies that might even be damaging to social cohesion or involve conflicts. Some housing policies may lead to polarisation or stigmatisation of certain groups.

55.     Strategies for the promotion of social cohesion should include housing policy, which should give special consideration to vulnerable groups.

56.     Besides housing market factors, the extent and the nature of housing problems depends on the efficiency of the existing welfare system. With a poorly functioning welfare system and inefficient safety net, fewer people will be able to afford adequate housing, thus the housing policy will have more tasks to solve. On the other hand, an efficient welfare system might partially reduce the tasks of housing policies. Housing policy is connected to other public policies (such as employment policies or urban development policies), and its potential contribution to social cohesion depends partly on how much is solved by those other policies.

57.     In order to promote social cohesion, all housing policies should give special attention to vulnerable groups:

–     housing policy instruments should provide for measures ensuring effective access to housing policy benefits by vulnerable groups;

–     the public policies should be designed in a way which increases the supply of housing for vulnerable groups and facilitates the creation of socially mixed neighbourhoods;

–     housing policies should include provision of information and counselling to vulnerable groups, in order to draw maximum benefits from the available programmes. Housing assistance programmes may fail because low-income households, who are target beneficiaries, may lack information of wider options;

– segregation of people with special needs should be avoided and they should be provided with appropriate social services in order to facilitate their participation in the community.

58. Housing policies aimed at the special needs of vulnerable groups have to contribute to the formation of healthy and inclusive neighbourhoods that provide access to the basic services for all sectors of society.

59. Area-based targeting may be necessary, in order to increase the quality of life of people living in these areas, limit the segregation processes, and allow for a mixed neighbourhood. Creation of mixed neighbourhoods is desirable as long as it does not lead to exclusion of persons on low incomes.

60. Measures to counteract discrimination on an individual basis when planning and managing housing estates, neighbourhoods and areas should be implemented and monitored.

61. Whenever housing policies in general and housing measures for vulnerable groups in particular are designed, a prior assessment and evaluation of the consequences for social cohesion should be made.

62. Monitoring and evaluation of housing policies for vulnerable groups should include an assessment of the effects on social cohesion. For this purpose, appropriate indicators should be developed, statistical information should be collected on a regular basis, and research on this issue should be carried out.

## 7.4    References

Åhrén, P. (2004): "'Housing allowances' in Lujanen", *Housing and housing policy in the Nordic Countries,* Nordic Council of Ministers, Copenhagen.

Asselin, A., Tom, S. and Streich P.P. (2002): "Canada Mortgage and Housing Corporation", *Review of Finland's Housing policy.*

Balchin, P. (ed.) (1996): *Housing Policy in Europe,* Routledge, London.

Berner, E. (2001): "Learning from informal markets: innovative approaches to land and housing provision", *Development in Practice,* Volume 11, Nos. 2&3, pp. 292-307, May 2001.

Boelhouwer, P. (2000): *Financing the Social Rented Sector in Western Europe,* Delft University Press, Delft.

Boelhouwer, P. and Elsinga, M. (2002): "Evaluation of Finnish housing finance and support systems", Ministry of the Environment, Helsinki.

Bradshaw, J. and Finch, N. (2003): "Housing benefits in the child benefit package in 22 countries", paper of the Housing Studies Association Spring Conference, University of York, 2 April 2003.

Bramley, G. and Morgan, J. (1998): "Low cost home ownership initiatives in the UK", *Housing Studies,* Vol. 13, No. 4, pp. 467-586.

Bratt, R. (2003): "Housing for very low-income households: the record of President Clinton, 1993-2000", *Housing Studies,* Vol. 18, No. 4, pp. 607-635, July 2003.

Brzeski, W.J. (2003): "Dilemmas and challenges of the post-soviet housing reforms", manuscript.

Buckley, R., Karaguishiyeva, G., Van Order, R. and Vecvagare, L. (2003): "Comparing Mortgage Credit Risk Policies: An Options Based Approach", World Bank Policy Research Working Paper 3047, May 2003.

Burchell R.W. and C. Galley, K. (2000): "Inclusionary Zoning: Pros and Cons", *New Century Housing,* Vol. 1, Issue 2.

Clapham, A. and Fitzgerald, R. (2004): "Early findings from a new approach to lender's mortgage insurance. Adequate and affordable housing for all", International Housing Research Conference, University of Toronto.

Conway, F.J. and Mikelsons, M. (1996): "A Review of Demand-Side Housing Subsidy Programs: The Case of Latin America", *Report 06623-000-00,* The Urban Institute, Washington, D.C.

Crook, A.D.H., Darke, R.A. and Disson, J.S. (1996): "Housing association investment on local authority estates", Joseph Rowntree Foundation Housing Research Findings No. 199, York, November 1996.

Cummings, J.L. and DiPasquale, D. (1999): "The Low-Income Housing Tax Credit: An Analysis of the First Ten Years", Housing Policy Debate, Vol. 10, Issue 2, pp. 251-307, Fannie Mae Foundation.

Čačić, R. (2003): "Housing in Croatia – efforts and results", presentation given at a high-level meeting of the Council of Europe, Paris, April 2004.

CBO (2004): "Estimating the value of subsidies for federal loans and loan guarantees", The Congress of the United States, Congressional Budget Office, August 2004.

DTLG (2001): "Delivering affordable housing through planning policy", Department for Transport, Local Government and the Regions.

Diamond, D.B. (1998): "Are Bausparkassen Appropriate Policy Instruments in Transition Countries?" December 1998.

Ditch, J., Lewis, A. and Wilcox, S. (2001): "Social Housing, Tenure and Housing Allowance: an International Review", study carried out by the Department for Work and Pensions, Social Policy, University of York.

Donner, C. (2000): "Housing Policies in the European Union (Theory and practice)".

Donnison, D. and Ungerson, C. (1982): Housing Policy, Penguin Books.

Doling, J. (1997): Comparative housing politics, London, Macmillan.

Doling, J. (2005): "Home Ownership in Europe: Contributing to Growth and Employment", keynote speech at the European Network of Housing Research, International Housing Conference on Housing in Europe: "New Challenges and Innovations in Tomorrow's Cities", Reykjavik, Iceland, 29 June to 3 July 2005.

Dragana, A., "Housing Conditions and Housing Policy in Belgium", Population and Social Policy Consultants (PSPC) (http://www.iccr-international.org/impact/docs/housing-policies-be.doc).

Dübel, H.J. (2000): "Separating Homeownership Subsidies from Finance: Traditional Mortgage Market Policies, Recent Reform Experiences and Lessons for Subsidy Reform", Land and Real Estate Studies, The World Bank, June 2000.

Dübel, H.J. (2003): "Financial, fiscal and housing policy aspects of Contract Savings for Housing (CSH) in Transition Countries – the Cases of Czech

Republic and Slovakia", *Financial Services Consultant,* The World Bank, Berlin, June 2003.

Dzepar-Ganibegovic, N. (2003): "An Outline of Pilot Project for Social Housing", Canton Sarajevo UNECE Workshop on Social Housing, Prague, 19 to 20 May 2003.

EBRD (2002): "Private Finance for Public Housing".

ECB (2003): "Structural Factors in the EU Housing Markets", European Central Bank, March 2003.

Elbers, A. (2003): "Financing of Social Housing in the Netherlands", UNECE Workshop on Social Housing "Sustainable Development of Social Housing: Financial Sustainability", Prague, 19-20 May 2003.

Enberg, L. (2000): "Social Housing in Denmark", *Research papers No. 6/00,* Department of Social Sciences, Institute for Samfundsvidenskab og Erhversokonomi.

Esping-Andersen, G. (1996): "Welfare States in Transition. Social Security in the New Global Economy", Sage, London.

Fallis, G. (1990): "The Optimal Design of Housing Allowances", *Journal of Urban Economics,* Vol. 27, Issue 3, pp. 381-397.

Familjeutredningen (2001): "Ur fattigdomsfällan", *SOU,* 2001:24, Stockholm, (The government enquiry on families: Out of the poverty trap).

Ferguson, B., and Navarrete, J. (2003): "New approaches to progressive housing in Latin America: A key to habitat programs and policy", *Habitat International,* Vol. 27, Issue 2, p. 319, June 2003.

Ferguson B., Rubinstein, J. and Dominguez, V. (1996): "The design of direct subsidy programs for housing in Latin America", *Review of urban & regional development studies,* Vol. 8, No. 2, July 1996, pp. 202-219.

Frank, D. (2004): "Housing Finance to improve the housing of low-income families: The example of the housing incentive system in Ecuador", Adequate and Affordable Housing for All, International Housing Research Conference, University of Toronto.

Gibb, K. (1996): "Housing Affordability: Key Issues and Policies", *Strategies for Housing and Social Integration in Cities,* OECD, pp. 147-192.

Gibb, K. (2002): "Trends and Change in Social Housing Finance and Provision within the European Union", *Housing Studies,* Vol. 17, No. 2, pp. 325-336.

Green, R.K. and Malpezzi, S. (2003): "A primer on U.S. Housing Markets and Housing Policy", *AREUEA Monograph Series No. 3,* Urban Institute Press, Washington.

Grigsby, W.G. and Bourassa, S.C. (2003): "Trying to Understand Low-income Housing Subsidies: Lessons from the United States", *Urban Studies,* Vol. 40, pp. 973-992, November 2003.

Haffner, M.E.A. and Oxley, M. J. (1999): "Housing Subsidies: Definitions and Comparisons", *Housing Studies,* Vol. 14, No. 2, pp. 145-162.

Hancock, K. and Munro, M. (1992): "Housing subsidies, inequality and affordability: evidence from Glasgow", *Fiscal Studies,* pp. 71-97.

Harloe, M. (1995): *The People's Home? Social Rented Housing in Europe and America,* Blackwell, Oxford.

Hegedüs, J. (2003): "Dilemmas in Social Housing Policy in Hungary after the Transition", MRI.

Hegedüs, J. and Teller, N. (2003): "Management of the Housing Stock in South-Eastern Europe", Council of Europe Development Bank, World Bank, High-Level Conference on Housing Reforms in South-Eastern Europe, 23-24 April 2003, Paris.

Hegedüs, J. and Teller, N. (2005): "Development of the Housing Allowance Programmes in Hungary in the Context of CEE Transitional Countries", *European Journal of Housing Policy,* Vol. 5, Issue 2, pp. 187-209.

Hegedüs, J. and Teller, N. (2006): "Work Package 4: Housing and territorial development", ESPON 1.4.2, Preparatory Study on Social Aspects of EU Territorial Development, Final Report, draft (manuscript).

Hoek-Smit, M.C. and Diamond, D. (2003): "The Design and Implementation of Subsidies for Housing Finance", prepared for the World Bank Seminar on Housing Finance, 10-13 March 2003.

Holmans, A., Scanlon, K. and Whitehead, C. (2002): "Fiscal Policy Instruments to Promote Affordable Housing", *Research Report VII,* Cambridge Center for Housing and Planning Research, Cambridge.

Howenstine, E.J. (1986): "Housing vouchers", Centre for Urban Policy Research, Rutgers University, New Brunswick, NJ.

Hughes, G. (1979): "Housing income and subsidies", *Fiscal Studies,* Vol. 1, No. 8, pp. 20-38.

Hulse, K. (2001): "Demand Subsidies for Private Renters: A Comparative Review. Our Homes, Our Communities, Our Future", National Housing Conference 2001, Brisbane, Australia.

Hulse, K. (2002): "Demand Subsidies for Private Renters: A Comparative Review", Australian Housing and Urban Research Institute, Swinburne-Monash AHURI Research Centre, September 2002.

Kahrik, A., Köre, J., Hendrikon, M. and Allsaar, I. (2003): "From a state controlled to a *Laissez-Faire* Housing system (local government and housing in Estonia)", *Housing Policy: An End Or A New Beginning?*, ed. M. Lux, LGI Books, Open Society Institute, 2003.

Katsura, H.M. and Romanik, C.T. (2002): "Ensuring Access to Essential Services: Demand-Side Housing Subsidies", Social Protection Unit, Human Development Network, December 2002, The World Bank.

Kemp, P.A. (1990): "Income Related Assistance with Housing Costs: a Cross National Comparison", *Urban Studies,* Vol. 27, pp. 795-808.

Kemp, P.A. (1997): "A comparative study of housing allowances", Department of Social Security, London.

Kemp, P., Wilcox, S. and Rhodes, D. (2002): "Housing Benefit reform: Next steps", Joseph Rowntree Foundation.

Kleinhans, R. (2004): "Social implications of housing diversification in urban renewal: A review of recent literature", *Journal of Housing and the Built Environment,* Vol. 19, pp. 367-390, Kluwer Academic Publishers, The Netherlands.

Laferrère, A. and le Blanc, D. (2004): "Gone with the Windfall: How Do Housing Allowances Affect Student Co-residence?", *CESifo Economic Studies,* Vol. 50, 3/2004, pp. 451-477.

Lea, M.J. and Renaud, B. (1994): "Contract Savings for Housing: Suitability to TSE Financial Reforms", World Bank, November 1994.

Lind, H. (1999): "Rent regulation: A conceptual and comparative analysis", Division of Building and Real Estate Economics, Royal Institute of Technology, October 1999.

Lowe, S. (2004): *Housing Policy Analysis: British Housing in Cultural and Comparative Context,* Palgrave Macmillan.

Lux, M. (2003): "State and Local Government: How to Improve the Partnership", *Housing Policy: An End Or A New Beginning?,* ed. M. Lux, LGI Books, Open Society Institute.

Lykova, T. (2003): "Social Housing in Russia: Income-Oriented Provision of Housing or Income-oriented Rent Policies? Current State and Further Prospects", presentation for the American Real Estate and Urban Economics Association Conference, Krakow, June 2003.

Maclennan, D., Muellbauer, J. and Stephens, M. (1998): "Asymmetries in housing and Financial Market Institutions and EMU", *Oxford Review of Economic Policy*, Vol. 14, Issue 1, pp. 54-80.

Maclennan, D., Stephens, M. and Kemp, P. (1997): "Housing Policy in the EU Member States", European Parliament Directorate General for Research Social Affairs Series Working Document 14, Luxembourg, European Parliament.

Martin, G. (2001): "Swamps and alligators: The future for low-cost home-ownership", Joseph Rowntree Foundation.

Mayo, S.K. (1999): "Subsidies in Housing", *Sustainable Development Department Technical Papers Series,* Inter-American Development Bank, Washington, D. C.

Murie et al. (2003): "Large Housing Estates in Europe. General Developments and Theoretical Backgrounds", *RESTATE Report 1,* Faculty of Geosciences, Utrecht University, Utrecht.

Ministry of the Environment (2002): "Evaluation of Finnish housing finance and support systems", Helsinki.

Murray, M. (1994): "How inefficient are multiple in-kind transfers?" *Economic injury,* Vol. 32, No. 2, pp. 209-227.

National board of housing, building and planning (2005): "Welcome to the housing market!" an intermediate report on segregation, Karlskrona, Sweden (in Swedish).

Nordvik, V. and Åhrén, P.P. (2004): "The Norwegian Housing Allowances – Efficiency and Effects", paper presented at the ENHR Conference in Cambridge in July 2004.

O'Sullivan, A.J. (1984): "Misconception in the current housing subsidy debate", *Policy and Politics,* Vol. 12, No. 2, pp. 119-144.

O'Sullivan, A.J. (1986): "The theory and measurement of tax expenditures and their impact", G.A.

OECD (1996): "Strategies for housing and social integration in cities".

Oxley, M. (2000): "The Future of Social Housing Learning from Europe", London, Institute for Public Policy Research.

Pascariu, S. and Stanculescu, M. (2003): "Management Improvement and Quality Standard Challenge (Local Government and Housing in Romania)", *Housing Policy: An End Or A New Beginning?*, ed. M. Lux, LGI Books, Open Society Institute.

Pedersen, R.B. (2002): "Co-operative Housing – the Norwegian Model", presentation at at a colloquium on contribution of the Co-operative Sector to Housing Development, The Federation of Co-operative Housing Associations (NBBL), 27-28 June 2002, Ankara, Turkey.

Pomeroy, S. (2004): "Attracting Private Sector Financing in Affordable Housing", Focus Consulting, Inc.Tri-Country Conference.

Press releases of DG Competition and copies of the Official Journal of the European Union via http://ec.europa.eu/comm/competition/index_en. html.

Priemus, H. (2000): "Rent Subsidies in the USA and Housing Allowances in the Netherlands: Worlds Apart", *International Journal of Urban and Regional Research,* Vol. 24, Issue 3, pp. 700-712.

Priemus, H. (2003): "Dutch Housing Associations: Current Developments and Debates", *Housing Studies,* Vol. 18, No. 3, pp. 327-351, May 2003.

Priemus, H. (2004): "Dutch housing allowances: social housing at risk", *International Journal of Urban and Regional Research,* Vol. 28, Issue 3, p. 706.

Priemus, H. and Boelhouwer, P. (1999): "Social Housing Finance in Europe: Trends and Opportunities", *Urban Studies,* Vol. 36, No. 4, pp. 633-646.

Priemus, H. and Dieleman, F. (1999): "Social Housing Finance in the European Union Developments and Prospects", *Urban Studies,* Vol. 36, No. 4, pp. 623-633.

Scanlon, K. and Whitehead, C. (2004): "Housing tenure and mortgage systems: A survey of 19 countries", London School of Economics.

Schroder, M. (2002): "Does housing assistance perversely affect self-sufficiency?", *Journal of Housing Economics,* Vol. 11, pp. 381-417.

Stephens, M. (2004): "An Exploration of the Behavioral Implications of Shifting from Housing Allowances to Income Subsidies", paper presented at the ENHR Conference in Cambridge, July 2004.

Stephens M., Burns N. and MacKay L. (2002): *Social market or safety net? British social rented housing in a European context,* The Policy Press.

Stephens, M. and Steen, G. (2004): "An exploration of the behavioural implications of shifting from housing allowances to income subsidies", paper for 2004 ENHR Conference, Cambridge.

Struyk, R. and Kolodeznikova, A. (1999): "Needs-based Targeting without Knowing Household Incomes: How Would it work in Russia?" *Urban Studies,* Vol. 36, No. 11, pp. 1875-1889.

Taffin, C. (2003): "Sustainable Development of Social Housing: Financial Sustainability", UNECE Workshop on Social Housing, Prague, 19-20 May 2003.

Taffin, C. (2006): "Financing of social housing", *Guidelines for social housing,* UN, New York and Geneva.

The Housing Corporation (2003): "Black and minority ethnic housing associations: the challenge of growth and viability. An assessment of governance, management and regulatory responses to the challenge of growth and viability since 1988" (http://www.monitoring-group.co.uk/News%20and%20Campaigns/news-stories/2003/Housing/R69_bme_housing_associations.pdf).

Tshenkova, S. (2003): "Housing Policy in Latvia: Muddling Through", paper prepared for the American Real Estate and Urban Economics Association Conference, Krakow, June 2003.

Turner, B., (1997): "Social Housing Finance in Sweden", *Urban Studies,* Vol. 36, No. 4, pp. 683-697, 1999.

Turner, B., Hegedüs, J. and Tosics, I. (eds) (1992): *The Reform of Housing in Eastern Europe and the Soviet Union,* London, Routledge.

Turner, B., Jakobsson J. and Whitehead, C.M.E. (1996): "Comparative Housing Finance", *Bostadspolitik 2000 (Housing Policy 2000),* appendix to the report from the Housing Policy Committee, SOU 1996, 156, Fritzes, Stockholm.

Turner, B. and Whitehead, C.M.E. (2002): "Reducing Housing Subsidy: Swedish Housing Policy in an International Context", *Urban Studies,* Vol. 39, No. 2, pp. 201-217.

Uchman, R. and Adamski, J. (2003): "How to meet market rules and social goals for Housing?", *Housing Policy: An End Or A New Beginning?,* ed. M. Lux, LGI Books, Open Society Institute.

UNECE (2003): "Social Housing in the ENECE Region", discussion paper prepared by the UNECE secretariat in co-operation with the European

Liaison Committee for Social Housing (CECODHAS), Workshop on Social Housing, UNECE, Prague, 19-20 May 2003.

Węcławowicz et al. (2004): "Large housing Estates in Poland: Policies and Practices", *RESTATE Report 3f,* Faculty of Geosciences, University of Utrecht, Utrecht.

Wilcox, S. (2003): "Can work – can't buy: Local measures of the ability of working households to become home owners", Joseph Rowntree Foundation.

Wood, G.A. (ed.) (1986): "Tax Policies and Urban Housing Markets", OECD, Paris.

World Bank (1993): "Housing: Enabling Markets to Work", *Urban Development,* World Bank Policy Paper, World Bank, Washington, D.C.

World Bank (2000): "Housing Microfinance Initiatives, Synthesis and Regional Summary: Asia, Latin America and Sub-Saharan Africa with Selected Case Studies", The Center for Urban Development Studies, Harvard University Graduate School of Design, commissioned by Development Alternatives Inc. (DAI), USAID MicroEnterprise Best Practices (http://wbln0018.worldbank.org/html/FinancialSectorWeb.nsf/ (attachmentweb)/HousingMicrofinanceInitiativesHarvardGSD000501/ $FILE/Housing+Microfinance+Initiatives+HarvardGSD+000501.pdf).

Zapletalova, J., Antalikova, M. and Smatanova, E. (2003): "The Role of Self-government in Housing Development in Slovakia", *Housing Policy: An End Or A New Beginning?,* ed. M. Lux, LGI Books, Open Society Institute.

Zawislak, M. (2003): "Expanding 'true social' sector in Poland", UNECE Workshop on Social Housing, Prague, 19-20 May 2003.

# Sales agents for publications of the Council of Europe
# Agents de vente des publications du Conseil de l'Europe

**BELGIUM/BELGIQUE**
La Librairie Européenne -
The European Bookshop
Rue de l'Orme, 1
B-1040 BRUXELLES
Tel.: +32 (0)2 231 04 35
Fax: +32 (0)2 735 08 60
E-mail: order@libeurop.be
http://www.libeurop.be

Jean De Lannoy
Avenue du Roi 202 Koningslaan
B-1190 BRUXELLES
Tel.: +32 (0)2 538 43 08
Fax: +32 (0)2 538 08 41
E-mail: jean.de.lannoy@dl-servi.com
http://www.jean-de-lannoy.be

**CANADA**
Renouf Publishing Co. Ltd.
1-5369 Canotek Road
OTTAWA, Ontario K1J 9J3, Canada
Tel.: +1 613 745 2665
Fax: +1 613 745 7660
Toll-Free Tel.: (866) 767-6766
E-mail: order.dept@renoufbooks.com
http://www.renoufbooks.com

**CZECH REPUBLIC/**
**RÉPUBLIQUE TCHÈQUE**
Suweco CZ, s.r.o.
Klecakova 347
CZ-180 21 PRAHA 9
Tel.: +420 2 424 59 204
Fax: +420 2 848 21 646
E-mail: import@suweco.cz
http://www.suweco.cz

**DENMARK/DANEMARK**
GAD
Vimmelskaftet 32
DK-1161 KØBENHAVN K
Tel.: +45 77 66 60 00
Fax: +45 77 66 60 01
E-mail: gad@gad.dk
http://www.gad.dk

**FINLAND/FINLANDE**
Akateeminen Kirjakauppa
PO Box 128
Keskuskatu 1
FIN-00100 HELSINKI
Tel.: +358 (0)9 121 4430
Fax: +358 (0)9 121 4242
E-mail: akatilaus@akateeminen.com
http://www.akateeminen.com

**FRANCE**
La Documentation française
(diffusion/distribution France entière)
124, rue Henri Barbusse
F-93308 AUBERVILLIERS CEDEX
Tél.: +33 (0)1 40 15 70 00
Fax: +33 (0)1 40 15 68 00
E-mail: commande@ladocumentationfrancaise.fr
http://www.ladocumentationfrancaise.fr

Librairie Kléber
1 rue des Francs Bourgeois
F-67000 STRASBOURG
Tel.: +33 (0)3 88 15 78 88
Fax: +33 (0)3 88 15 78 80
E-mail: francois.wolfermann@librairie-kleber.fr
http://www.librairie-kleber.com

**GERMANY/ALLEMAGNE**
**AUSTRIA/AUTRICHE**
UNO Verlag GmbH
August-Bebel-Allee 6
D-53175 BONN
Tel.: +49 (0)228 94 90 20
Fax: +49 (0)228 94 90 222
E-mail: bestellung@uno-verlag.de
http://www.uno-verlag.de

**GREECE/GRÈCE**
Librairie Kauffmann s.a.
Stadiou 28
GR-105 64 ATHINAI
Tel.: +30 210 32 55 321
Fax.: +30 210 32 30 320
E-mail: ord@otenet.gr
http://www.kauffmann.gr

**HUNGARY/HONGRIE**
Euro Info Service kft.
1137 Bp. Szent István krt. 12.
H-1137 BUDAPEST
Tel.: +36 (06)1 329 2170
Fax: +36 (06)1 349 2053
E-mail: euroinfo@euroinfo.hu
http://www.euroinfo.hu

**ITALY/ITALIE**
Licosa SpA
Via Duca di Calabria, 1/1
I-50125 FIRENZE
Tel.: +39 0556 483215
Fax: +39 0556 41257
E-mail: licosa@licosa.com
http://www.licosa.com

**MEXICO/MEXIQUE**
Mundi-Prensa México, S.A. De C.V.
Río Pánuco, 141 Delegacíon Cuauhtémoc
06500 MÉXICO, D.F.
Tel.: +52 (01)55 55 33 56 58
Fax: +52 (01)55 55 14 67 99
E-mail: mundiprensa@mundiprensa.com.mx
http://www.mundiprensa.com.mx

**NETHERLANDS/PAYS-BAS**
De Lindeboom Internationale Publicaties b.v.
M.A. de Ruyterstraat 20 A
NL-7482 BZ HAAKSBERGEN
Tel.: +31 (0)53 5740004
Fax: +31 (0)53 5729296
E-mail: books@delindeboom.com
http://www.delindeboom.com

**NORWAY/NORVÈGE**
Akademika
Postboks 84 Blindern
N-0314 OSLO
Tel.: +47 2 218 8100
Fax: +47 2 218 8103
E-mail: support@akademika.no
http://www.akademika.no

**POLAND/POLOGNE**
Ars Polona JSC
25 Obroncow Street
PL-03-933 WARSZAWA
Tel.: +48 (0)22 509 86 00
Fax: +48 (0)22 509 86 10
E-mail: arspolona@arspolona.com.pl
http://www.arspolona.com.pl

**PORTUGAL**
Livraria Portugal
(Dias & Andrade, Lda.)
Rua do Carmo, 70
P-1200-094 LISBOA
Tel.: +351 21 347 42 82 / 85
Fax: +351 21 347 02 64
E-mail: info@livrariaportugal.pt
http://www.livrariaportugal.pt

**RUSSIAN FEDERATION/**
**FÉDÉRATION DE RUSSIE**
Ves Mir
9a, Kolpacnhyi per.
RU-101000 MOSCOW
Tel.: +7 (8)495 623 6839
Fax: +7 (8)495 625 4269
E-mail: orders@vesmirbooks.ru
http://www.vesmirbooks.ru

**SPAIN/ESPAGNE**
Mundi-Prensa Libros, s.a.
Castelló, 37
E-28001 MADRID
Tel.: +34 914 36 37 00
Fax: +34 915 75 39 98
E-mail: libreria@mundiprensa.es
http://www.mundiprensa.com

**SWITZERLAND/SUISSE**
Van Diermen Editions – ADECO
Chemin du Lacuez 41
CH-1807 BLONAY
Tel.: +41 (0)21 943 26 73
Fax: +41 (0)21 943 36 05
E-mail: info@adeco.org
http://www.adeco.org

**UNITED KINGDOM/ROYAUME-UNI**
The Stationery Office Ltd
PO Box 29
GB-NORWICH NR3 1GN
Tel.: +44 (0)870 600 5522
Fax: +44 (0)870 600 5533
E-mail: book.enquiries@tso.co.uk
http://www.tsoshop.co.uk

**UNITED STATES and CANADA/**
**ÉTATS-UNIS et CANADA**
Manhattan Publishing Company
468 Albany Post Road
CROTTON-ON-HUDSON, NY 10520, USA
Tel.: +1 914 271 5194
Fax: +1 914 271 5856
E-mail: Info@manhattanpublishing.com
http://www.manhattanpublishing.com

**Council of Europe Publishing/Editions du Conseil de l'Europe**
F-67075 Strasbourg Cedex
Tel.: +33 (0)3 88 41 25 81 – Fax: +33 (0)3 88 41 39 10 – E-mail: publishing@coe.int – Website: http://book.coe.int